M000309130

The Secret of Inner Peace

The Secret of INNER PEACE

Discourses on Spirituality

Swami Ramakrishnananda Puri

Mata Amritanandamayi Center, San Ramon
California, United States

The Secret Of Inner Peace
Discourses on Spirituality
by Swami Ramakrishnananda Puri

Published by:
Mata Amritanandamayi Center
P.O. Box 613
San Ramon, CA 94583
United States

Copyright © 2006 by Mata Amritanandamayi Center
All rights reserved. No part of this publication may be stored in a retrieval system, transmitted, reproduced, transcribed or translated into any language, in any form, by any means without the prior agreement and written permission of the publisher.

In India:
www.amritapuri.org
inform@amritapuri.org

In Europe:
www.amma-europe.org

In US:
www.amma.org

Dedication

Amma, my life is no longer empty.
I am filled with a deep peace.
Knowing that your holy feet
are deeply imprinted in my heart
brings tears of joy to my eyes.

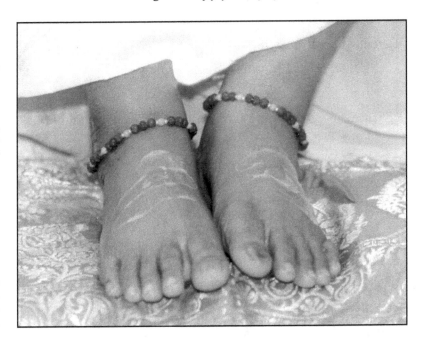

I humbly offer this book at the lotus feet of my beloved
Satguru, Sri Mata Amritanandamayi Devi

Contents

Preface

Last year, when I began writing *The Blessed Life*, it seemed that I would have plenty of time to complete the book before my intended release date of Amma's 52nd birthday. Then, one after another, things started coming up. I had to visit several tsunami relief sites in Tamil Nadu and Sri Lanka. I also had to hold programs at a few of Amma's schools and colleges in different parts of South India. On top of that I was scheduled to leave for an extended trip to South America. A few days before my departure, I told Amma that it seemed I would be unable to finish the book on time. To this Amma replied simply, "Don't worry." Hearing this I thought maybe Amma meant that I shouldn't worry about being unable to finish the book. At the same time I realized it could also mean that I should not worry because Amma would help me to achieve my goal. Optimistically, I took the second interpretation as the correct one. I told this to the brahmachari who was assisting me in editing the book. He said, "Swamiji, if you were writing an article, I would agree with you. But since you are, after all, writing a book, I think it might be better to take the first meaning and not worry about completing the book. That way you can focus on your other work in peace."

With Amma's grace, however, I was able to finish the book the night before I left for South America. As I was writing the book's closing sentences, the following verses from the *Gita Dhyanam* came to mind.

mūkaṁ karoti vācālaṁ
paṅguṁ laṅghataye girim
yat kṛpā tam ahaṁ vande
paramānanda mādhavaṁ

I bow down to Madhava,
the Source of Supreme Bliss,
whose grace makes the mute eloquent speakers,
and the lame cross mountains.

Today, I feel those words are just as appropriate to the writing of this book, which was done under similar time constraints and with even more apparent obstacles to completion. That you hold it in your hands is a tribute to Amma's grace alone, of which I have always aspired to become a pure instrument.

Swami Ramakrishnananda Puri
Amritapuri
27 September 2006

Introduction

Once a man heard a radio personality declare, "The way to achieve inner peace is to finish all the things you've started and never finished." Taking these words to heart, he looked around his house to see all the things he had started but never finished. He proceeded to finish off a bottle of champagne, a six-pack of beer, a package of chocolate chip cookies, the remaining three quarters of a blueberry cheesecake and a box of gourmet chocolates. Thinking he'd discovered a revelation, he decided to call all his friends and tell them about the brilliant new strategy. But on his way to the phone he lost consciousness, and when he woke up he was staring up at the bright lights of the emergency room. Like this, we may have had many false starts and wrong turns on the path to inner peace. If we really want inner peace, we should look at the lives and teachings of the ones who have attained it.

We live in the same world as the spiritual masters and come up against the same difficulties in life, yet they are peaceful and content while we remain restless and dissatisfied. Once, a very successful scientist came to meet Amma. When Amma asked him about his family's well-being, the scientist burst into tears. He explained that his son had not been admitted to the college of his choice. As a result the scientist had been spending sleepless nights agonizing over his son's future. Though the scientist was an intellectual giant, he lacked the capacity to face life's challenges with equipoise.

It might be difficult for readers to imagine that when I first met Amma twenty-nine years ago, she was living outdoors, sleeping beneath the stars, and living virtually like a homeless person. In fact, she had already been living like that for a long time. A few years later, after the first group of *brahmacharis* (celibate disciples) came to settle there, a small hut was constructed. At that time, I never imagined that from such humble origins would emerge a massive spiritual and social service organization touching tens of millions of people around the world that would create positive global impact in so many ways.

Sometimes people ask Amma, "You have achieved so much in such a short span of time. How do you feel about your accomplishments?"

Amma replies, "I don't feel anything about them. The world may praise me or criticize me. Either way, I am not affected. I am not looking for appreciation or recognition. I have already offered myself to the world, and I will continue to serve humanity in whatever way possible until my last breath."

Amma was at peace then, when she had neither a roof over her head nor a friend in the world, and she is at peace now, as one of the most widely recognized and respected spiritual leaders and humanitarians in the world. Amma says that real spiritual achievement is the ability to maintain mental equanimity in all circumstances—to never lose the inner peace that is our real nature and true home. A fish floundering on land may not know or believe that there is water within its reach; as a result, it suffers. Similarly, as long as we remain unaware that the source of all peace and contentment lies within us, we will continue to suffer.

Once, a man fell out of a second-story window. He was lying on the ground with a big crowd gathered around him when a police officer walked over and asked, "What happened?"

"I don't know," the man on the ground answered. "I just got here."

We may laugh at the man's folly, but as human beings, our situation is not so different. What do we know about how we got here, where we came from, or where we are going? What do we really know about who we are? Recognizing our own foolishness is a great step toward wisdom, insofar as it makes us receptive to the guidance of a true spiritual master.

Through grace, guidance and the example of his[1] own life, the spiritual master leads us to the realization that, in truth, we are not waves destined to crash helplessly against the shore and disappear forever. Rather, we are the ocean itself. We ourselves *are* the supreme bliss and everlasting peace for which we have been searching—for this is the nature of our True Self, the all-pervading Supreme Consciousness: the *Atman*.

There has never been a more patient, loving and accessible guide than we have in Amma, whose every word, every action, every breath is a testament to this Truth. Looking at Amma's life, we can learn how to make the most of our own life—we can learn the secret of inner peace.

---

[1] This book primarily uses the masculine pronoun, in keeping with convention and to avoid the clumsiness of such constructions as 'he or she' or 'him or her.' Needless to say, God is neither male nor female, but transcends gender. In other cases where the context does not clearly indicate the gender, including those referring to the guru, the masculine pronoun should be read as gender-inclusive.

Amma's Life:
In Her Own Words

"As long as there is enough strength in these hands to reach out to those who come to Amma, to place her hand on a crying person's shoulder, Amma will continue to do so... To lovingly caress people, to console and wipe their tears until the end of this mortal frame—this is Amma's wish."

—Amma

Born in a remote coastal village in Kerala, Southern India, Amma says that she always knew there was a higher reality beyond this changing world of names and forms. Even as a child, Amma expressed love and compassion to everyone. Amma says, "An unbroken stream of love flows from Amma to all beings in the universe. This is Amma's inborn nature."

About her early years, Amma says, "Right from childhood, Amma wondered why people in the world have to suffer. Why must they be poor? Why must they starve? For example, in the area where Amma grew up, the people are fishermen. Some days they go out fishing but don't catch anything. And because of this, there are times when they have to go without food—sometimes for several days. Amma became very close with these villagers and had many chances to learn about the nature of the world by observing their lives and difficulties.

"Amma used to do all the household chores, one of which was feeding the many family cows and goats. To do so, every day she had to go to thirty or—on some days even sixty–houses in the neighborhood and collect tapioca peels and other such leftovers. Whenever she went to visit these houses, she always found that people were

13

suffering—sometimes due to old age, sometimes poverty, sometimes disease. Amma would sit with them, listen to their problems, share their suffering and pray for them.

"Whenever she had time, Amma used to bring these people to her parents' house. There, she would give them a hot bath and feed them, and occasionally she even took things from her own house to give to these starving families.

"Amma observed that when children are young, they depend upon their parents, so they pray that their parents live for a long time and that they do not become sick. But when these same children grow up, they feel that their parents, who are now old, are a burden. They think, 'Why should I do all this work for my parents?' Feeding them, washing their clothes and treating them with care becomes a burden to these same children who previously prayed that their parents would live for a long time. Seeing this, a question arose from within her: 'Why are there so many contradictions in this world? Why is there no real love? What is the real cause of all this suffering and what is the solution?'"

Amma says, "Immediately the answer came from within that the suffering of humanity was due to people's karma, the fruit of their past deeds. But Amma was not satisfied with this. She thought to herself: 'If it is their karma to suffer, isn't it your *dharma*[2] to help them?' If somebody falls into a deep pit, is it correct to simply walk by, saying, 'Oh, it is their karma to suffer that way'? No, it is our duty to help them climb out.

"Even from early childhood, Amma knew that God—the Self, the Supreme Power—alone is Truth and that the world is not the absolute reality. Therefore she would spend long periods immersed

---

[2] In Sanskrit, dharma means "that which upholds (creation)." It is used to mean different things in different contexts, or more accurately, different aspects of the same thing. Here, the closest direct translation is "duty." Other meanings include: righteousness, harmony.

in deep meditation. Amma's parents and relatives didn't understand what was happening. Out of ignorance, they began scolding her and opposing her spiritual practices."

But Amma was immersed in the remembrance of God, totally unaffected by the criticism and chastisement of her family. During this time, Amma had to spend days and nights outside under the open sky. It was animals and birds that took care of her, bringing her food and stirring her from deep meditative states.

"Experiencing her oneness with all of creation, Amma realized that her purpose in life was to uplift ailing humanity. It was then that Amma started this spiritual mission, spreading this message of Truth, love and compassion throughout the world by receiving one and all."

Soon, more and more people wanted to experience Amma's unconditional love and compassion and started arriving from all corners of the world in the once sleepy, anonymous fishing village of Parayakadavu. Before long, those who wanted to experience Amma's unconditional love had to take a token and wait in a queue. Today, Amma spends most of the year traveling throughout India and the world in order to uplift suffering humanity through her words and the comfort of her loving embrace. Her ashram is home to 3,000 people, and thousands more visit every day from all over India and the world. Ashram residents and visitors alike are inspired by Amma's example and dedicate themselves to serving the world. Through Amma's vast network of charitable projects, they build homes for the homeless, give pensions to the destitute and provide medical care for the sick. Countless people all over the world are contributing to this loving endeavor—most recently, Amma received international acclaim for donating $1 million to the Bush-Clinton Katrina Fund for hurricane relief in the United States, and for dedicating more than $23 million for the relief and rehabilitation of tsunami victims in India, Sri Lanka and the Andaman & Nicobar Islands. When a journalist asked Amma how she could possibly pledge such a large sum for tsunami relief, Amma replied, "My children are my strength." She was not speaking only about the brahmacharis, brahmacharinis and other ashramites who work up to 15 hours a day without receiving any pay, dedicated to helping as many people as possible as quickly as possible. Referring to her millions of devotees around the world, Amma said, "I have many good children. They all do what they can." She went on to describe how even small children make dolls or statues and sell them so that they can give the earnings to their beloved Amma. "Some children," Amma said, "when presented with money on their birthday or when their parents tell them that they can have an ice cream, say that they would like to give that money to Amma instead, telling their parents how Amma can use it for supporting poor children. Other children come up to Amma and offer their savings, saying that it can be used to buy pens for poor students. Amma doesn't want to accept this—as other children who have nothing to offer may then feel sad—but when Amma sees the goodness of their hearts, she has no choice. The government alone cannot do everything. Would these children give this money to the government with the same love as they would give it to Amma?"

Amma has been showered with international honors: the Parliament of the World's Religions Centennial named her President of the Hindu faith, she delivered the keynote address at the United Nations' Millennium World Peace Summit, and she was presented with the 2002 Gandhi-King Award for Nonviolence. Most recently, Amma—along with 2005 Nobel Peace Prize winner Mohamed ElBaradei—was presented with the 2006 James Parks Morton Interfaith Award by the Interfaith Center of New York for her role as an outstanding spiritual leader and humanitarian. In presenting the award, the Interfaith Center cited in specific her ashram's massive relief work in the wake of the 2004 tsunami. While presenting the award, the Reverend James Parks Morton said to Amma, "You embody everything that we stand for."

"In the end," Amma says, "love is the only medicine that can heal the wounds of the world. In this universe, it is love that binds everything together. As this awareness dawns within us, all disharmony will cease. Abiding peace alone will reign." ❖

CHAPTER 1

Cultivating a Healthy Mind

"Difficulties strengthen the mind, as labor does the body."

– Seneca

When Amma first started visiting Japan, the United States, and many other developed countries almost twenty years ago, I was one of a small group of disciples accompanying her. It was my first time leaving India, and I was very impressed with what I saw. Everyone had computers, vacuum cleaners, washing machines—some people already had mobile phones. Now, of course, India is also a rapidly developing nation. But at that time, these sights were a wonder to me. Seeing the technological development and physical comforts prevailing in Western society, I thought, "This is verily heaven." I even thought that Amma need not have come to the West because people seemed to have everything they needed.

But when Amma's *darshan*[3] began, people began telling their problems to Amma. Often I was translating for them, and when

---

[3] Literally, "to see." It is traditionally used in the context of meeting a holy person, seeing an image of God, or having a vision of God. In this book, darshan refers to Amma's motherly embrace. About her darshan, Amma has said, "Amma's hugs and kisses should not be considered ordinary. When Amma embraces or kisses someone, it is a process of purification and inner healing. Amma is transmitting a part of her pure, vital energy into her children. It also allows them to experience true, unconditional love. When Amma holds someone, it can help to awaken the dormant

I heard their problems—drug addiction, teenage pregnancy, multiple divorces, depression—I was dumbfounded. Before coming to the West, I had thought depression was a weather phenomenon or an economic slump. I had never met anyone who had a psychiatrist; in the West, I found that even dogs had their own psychiatrists. I recalled the words of the Western philosopher Jean-Paul Sartre, who commented, "Everything has been figured out, except how to live." There was no doubt that the people in these countries were leading a comfortable external life, but internally they were undergoing a great deal of turmoil. Amma's love was a much-needed balm for their wounded hearts, and her spiritual guidance gave them the strength and confidence they needed to move forward in life.

In order to enjoy a peaceful life, we need to imbibe the spiritual principles as words to live by. This means giving up our attachments and expectations and understanding the changing nature of the world and people.

Many feel that spirituality is a nice philosophy, but that it has no relevance for the practical demands of daily life. We may wonder: what is the connection between spirituality and our day-to-day life? Suppose our leg is badly infected and we need an injection of antibiotics. The doctor need not put the syringe in our leg; he'll give us the injection in our arm. At that time, we don't protest, "Doctor, the problem is in my leg; why are you giving me an injection in my arm?" because we know that the medicine will travel through our blood and reach our infected leg. Similarly, though spiritual practices seem to have nothing to do with our day-to-day problems, in fact they are very closely connected. It is spirituality that prepares our mind to face the various

---

spiritual energy within them, which will eventually take them to the ultimate goal of Self-realization."

challenges of life. Just as medicine travels through the blood to the entire body, the medicine of spirituality travels through the mind and has a beneficial affect on every aspect of our life.

If we look closely, we can see that our life consists of nothing more than a series of varied experiences. All these experiences are possible only because of the mind. If the mind is not functioning, we do not experience anything. For example, when we are in deep sleep, even though the world still exists and people may talk and laugh and so many events might take place in our presence, we are not aware of it because the mind is not functioning. It is only when we wake up that we experience the world.

Because all our experiences are perceived through the mind, it is important that our mind is strong and healthy. There is a saying, "As the mind, so the man."—or, of course, so the woman. For example, if we are a dancer and the stage on which we are dancing is unstable, our performance, too, will be rickety. Similarly, our mind is the stage on which the drama of our life is unfolding. If the mind is unsteady, our life will reflect that. If the mind is steady and healthy, our life will be relatively happy and peaceful. It is the mind that makes us happy or unhappy, peaceful or tense, and it is spiritual understanding that helps us to cultivate a healthy mind and thereby experience more peace and contentment in life despite the changing nature of the world around us.

There is a story about a wealthy woman who lost all her money in a business deal. After telling her lover she was flat broke, she asked him, "My dear, in spite of the fact that I am no longer rich, will you still love me?"

"Certainly, honey," her lover assured her. "I will always love you—even though I will probably never see you again."

This is the nature of the world. Someone who loves us today may leave us tomorrow. We may not always get what we expect;

in fact, we may often get what we don't expect. Today we may be the very picture of health, while tomorrow we find that we have developed a debilitating disease. By highlighting such truths, spirituality prepares us to accept with equanimity the different situations life brings us.

Amma says that we may even have more bad experiences than good ones. The richness of our life is not determined by the number of pleasant experiences we have, but by how well we handle the unpleasant or challenging experiences. Sometimes, to prevent or cure an illness, we must drink a bitter-tasting medicine. Similarly, pleasant experiences improve the quality of our life, but handling the difficulties in life well is what helps us to develop inner strength.

There is a story about a certain court jester who went too far one day and insulted his king. The furious king sentenced the jester to be executed. His court urged the king to have mercy for this man who had served him well for so many years. After a time, the king relented only this much: he would allow the jester his choice as to how he would like to die. True to form, the jester replied, "If it's all the same to you, my lord, I'd like to die of old age."

Every situation in life presents us with a clear choice. We can either react—out of our ego, past experiences, attachments and negative emotions, or we can respond—out of our positive qualities like love, compassion, patience, and kindness. The key to responding rather than reacting to a given situation is acceptance. When we accept the situation as it is, we begin to see the hidden lessons and opportunities therein, and we can respond accordingly. However, most of us tend to react, and as a result we become frustrated, angry or depressed. Our lives then end up becoming a series of reactions, interspersed with a few peaceful moments when things temporarily go according to our expectations. In fact, we always have one problem or another, but in between big problems—when we have only smaller problems—we say that things are going our way.

There was a ten-year-old boy whose favorite hobby was martial arts. One day he was in a terrible auto accident, in which his left arm was damaged and had to be amputated. He could have reacted negatively to this misfortune and given up martial arts forever. Instead, he continued with his classes, and his judo master agreed to teach him a style of judo that could be performed with only one arm.

After three months, however, the boy had learned only one move. He asked his teacher to teach him some more moves. The judo master told him confidently that this was the only move he would need to know.

Soon after, the boy entered a tournament. The boy seemed very out-matched, as his opponent had two arms and was bigger and more experienced. But when the boy got his opportunity, he took the advantage and pinned the bigger boy using the move he had learned from his teacher.

On the ride home, the boy asked his teacher, "How was it that I was able to win with only one move?"

The master replied, "You have mastered one of the most difficult moves in all of judo. The only defense against that move is for your opponent to grab your left arm."

Because this boy chose to respond positively to the situation of losing his arm rather than reacting negatively, he found that in martial arts, at least, his biggest weakness had become his greatest strength.

Just like this boy, we can also choose to respond, rather than react, to all the situations in life. We have the freedom to do so, but most of the time we unwittingly forfeit this freedom, think-ing that life has dealt us a bad hand of cards.

Readers may be familiar with stories of the strict discipline which Amma's mother, Damayanti Amma, imposed on her as a child. Amma's mother, Damayanti Amma, told Amma that if she happened to step on a piece of waste paper, she should touch it and then touch her eyes as a sign of respect because any form of paper represents Saraswati, the goddess of learning. She would have to do the same if she stepped on the door-sill (because it takes one from one place to another place) and even if she stepped in cow dung (because the cow takes so little for itself and offers so much to the world). When Amma was a young girl, it was the custom not to light a fire in one's own house but to go to another house where the fire had already been lit; everyone in the village would light their own lamps from that one lamp. When Damayanti Amma sent Amma to go and light the lamp, she would tell her, "If you find any dirty dishes in that house, wash those dishes before returning. If the house needs cleaning, clean the house before you return." If a guest came to spend the night at the house, Amma's mother would tell her to spend the night in the front yard so the guest would have a room of his own. The guest would be fed first; Amma says that her mother did not worry about whether her children were fed, as long as the guest was given plenty to eat and made comfortable in every way; sometimes the children would only be given water. If Amma was grinding curries for the upcoming meal, Damayanti Amma would forbid her to speak until she was finished with the work, for fear that a drop of saliva would fall into the food.

Because Amma's mind was deeply immersed in spiritual prin-ciples, she was able to approach a seemingly negative situation in a positive light—despite all these severe restrictions, Amma says she never had any ill feelings toward her mother. Amma even sometimes refers to Damayanti Amma as her guru, commenting, "Though she didn't have any spiritual understanding, she was able to guide me." Amma says that she did not consider all these restrictions as different from spirituality; she felt that such rules help one to live with more awareness. Amma's ability to find a spiritual principle in each of her mother's instructions reflected the healthy state of her mind.

Once, a man was walking along the beach when he found a tarnished brass lamp lying in the sand. He picked it up and turned it over—it seemed to be empty. "Oh, why not," he said to himself, and, looking around to make sure no one was watching him, gave the lamp a quick rub.

Instantly, a genie appeared and thanked the man for letting him out. The genie said, "For your kindness I will grant you one wish, but only one."

The man thought for a minute and said, "I have always wanted to go to Hawaii, but have never been able to because I'm afraid of flying, and ships make me seasick. So, I wish for a bridge to be built from here to Hawaii."

The genie thought for a few minutes and said, "No, I don't think I can do that. Just think of all the work involved—the pilings needed to hold up the highway would have to reach the bottom of the ocean. Think of all the concrete you would need! Not to mention drainage systems, lighting... No, no, that's way too much to ask. Ask for something more reasonable."

The man thought for a minute. "Okay, how about this one? My wife and I are always quarrelling. Can you change her so that we can have a perfect marriage?"

The genie scratched his beard and mulled it over. Finally, he looked up and said, "Okay. Do you want that highway with two lanes or four?"

Amma says that we have a strong tendency to expect more out of the people in our life than they are capable of delivering. Amma compares this to looking at a frog and seeing an elephant. If we expect a frog to be able to perform the duties of an elephant, we will be sorely disappointed.

Only the proper understanding of spiritual principles will remove our unreasonable expectations about the world. Because Amma understands and accepts the nature of the world, she doesn't have unreasonable expectations about how people will treat her or what she can receive from the outside world. It is this clarity of vision that spirituality helps us to develop. We may never be able to see the world through Amma's eyes, but if we contemplate her teachings and follow her example to the best of our ability, we can certainly improve our vision. This will help us to enjoy more peace and contentment in our daily life and to remain focused on the real goal of human life—that of realizing our oneness with God, and with all of creation. ❖

CHAPTER 2

Subject and Object

*If you don't realize the source, you stumble in confusion and
sorrow. When you realize where you come from, you naturally
become tolerant, disinterested, amused, kindhearted as a
grandmother, dignified as a king. Immersed in the wonder
of the Tao, you can deal with whatever life brings you, and
when death comes, you are ready.*

—Tao Te Ching

One evening during India's festival season, a devotee was setting off spectacular fireworks at Amma's ashram. The sound
was deafening, and the sight spectacular. Midway through the
display, a hearing-impaired person emerged from his room and
asked, "Who is setting off all the lights?"

If the senses are not in good working order, we will not be
able to appreciate the objects of the senses. If our eyesight is poor,
even in bright light we will not be able to see clearly. When we
burn our tongue, we are not able to enjoy even the finest cuisine
in the world.

But for an experience to take place, it is not enough to have
perfectly functioning senses and for objects of experience to be
present. Every experience requires an experiencer, or subject of
experience. This subject is the mind.

Leaving the senses aside, then, every experience has two fundamental components: subject and object, or the mind and the

27

world around us. If we want to lead a peaceful and harmonious life, we need to deal with both the subject and objects of our experience. We are all familiar with trying to improve the objects of our experience. We are always searching for the nicest place to live, the highest-paying job, the tastiest food and the most attractive spouse, but if we do nothing to improve the subject of our experience-our own mind-we will not be able to enjoy even the most luxurious surroundings.[4] Amma says that the only difference between the rich and the poor is that the rich are crying in air-conditioned, carpeted rooms, while the poor are crying on the dirt floors of their huts. What we really need, Amma says, is to "air-condition the mind." If we succeed in this, we can be relatively peaceful wherever we are.

When our mind makes contact through the senses with the objects of the world around us, a three-step process takes place. First of all, our mind receives input from our senses. This information is then processed through our mind and intellect—an emotion, memory, desire or thought may arise. Finally, depending on the type of stimuli contacted and the condition of our mind and

---

[4] While most Western philosophers consider the mind as the subject, according to Vedanta, the mind is also an object, because we are aware of the condition of our mind-sad, happy, angry, calm, etc.-and whatever we are aware of is an object. However, Vedanta further says that while the mind is illumined by the Atman, the senses are illumined by the mind. Without the Atman, of course, the mind cannot function, but when the mind is not functioning--for example during deep sleep--though the Atman is still present, we do not experience anything. Just as the moon, itself illumined by the sun, sheds light onto the world throughout the night, so too the mind, illumined by the Atman, in turn illumines the senses. It is in this sense that the mind is being treated as a subject for the purposes of this chapter.

intellect, we send output—in the form of words or actions—in response to the stimuli.

The first step in optimizing this process is to be careful about the objects our senses make contact with. At least in our free time, most of us have a great deal of control over what kind of environment surrounds us. We can decide to go to a movie theater, a liquor store or a restaurant; we can just as easily visit a park, a zoo, a nursing home or a meditation center. Each environment will create a different impact on us, which will tend to produce corresponding output from us. By now, most of us have a good idea which environments will produce positive feelings like peace, calmness, love and compassion within us, and which environments tend to produce negative feelings like anxiety, lust, jealousy, frustration and anger. By maintaining continuous awareness, we can make the right choices about our environment and the objects with which our senses come into contact.

Of course, even if we make sure to receive positive stimuli from the outside world, we still do not have complete control over our mind. Even in a temple or a church, negative thoughts and feelings may arise. To illustrate this point, Amma often recounts the following anecdote.

In the old days, when Amma went for a tour of North India, she would take almost all the ashram residents with her, as there were only a handful of us. As the years have gone by, however, the number of brahmacharis and brahmacharinis at Amma's ashram has increased dramatically, and there are now so many that Amma cannot take all of them on tour with her at once. Nowadays, most of the ashram residents do only half the tour. On one such tour there was a brahmachari who would spend all his free time standing near Amma with a long face. Usually the mood is very cheerful around Amma as she gives darshan unless a devotee comes with a sad story. But amidst all the smiling faces this young man was always wearing a frown, and sometimes even shedding tears. One day Amma called him for darshan and asked him what the problem was. "I will have to leave Amma soon," he tearfully explained. "In just one more week I will have to return to the ashram." His group was doing the first half of the tour that year.

"But the same is true for all of these children," Amma said, gesturing to all the smiling faces around her. "Son, worrying about the future, you are unable to enjoy the present. Whereas, these children, enjoying the time they have with me and making the most of it, will be happy even when they have to go back, filled with the memories of these precious moments."

In fact, when the first group returned to the ashram and the second group joined the tour, Amma found that the despondent brahmachari had a counterpart in the second group. When she asked the second brahmachari what was wrong, he told Amma what was hanging heavily on his heart: "Amma didn't bring me for the first half of the tour." This thought troubled him for the remainder of the tour, and he was not able to enjoy himself at all.

In both cases, the young brahmacharis only needed to adjust the subject—their own mind—to enjoy the object, their experience of being on tour with Amma.

We cannot always exercise complete control over our external situation. We will inevitably be faced with unpleasant situations and environments that tend to bring out the worst in us. In such circumstances, even when a negative reaction arises within us, we need to be able to regulate our output so that we don't harm ourselves or anyone else with our words or actions.

Amma tells the following story. There were two brothers who, aside from being blood relatives, had nothing in common with one another. One of the men was a career criminal, in and out of jail his whole life, a deadbeat dad who had been through three failed marriages, and hopelessly addicted to drugs and alcohol. His brother, by contrast, was the vice-president of a successful company, who in his free time had founded a literacy campaign for the disadvantaged children in his community. Married to his high school sweetheart, together they had a child of their own and then decided to adopt two more. Struck by the remarkable difference, someone asked each of the two brothers the same question: "What is it that made you who you are today?"

The career criminal lamented, "It's all the fault of my father. He was an alcoholic and used to beat us for no reason at all. On top of that he never showed any love or affection to us. Now I have become just like him."

When the same question was put to the vice-president, he replied, "In fact, it is because of my father. His life was a failure in every respect. I swore that I would be different, that I would not repeat his mistakes. In a way, I am grateful to him—at least he showed me how *not* to live."

Both brothers received the negative input of an abusive father and a traumatic childhood—but their output was completely different. Everything depends on the condition of the processor—the mind.

There is a story in the epic *Srimad Bhagavatam* which can shed light on this point. Having received an omen that the eighth son born to his sister would kill him, the evil King Kamsa imprisoned his sister Devaki and her husband Vasudeva. Whenever a child was born to the couple, Kamsa took it by the feet and dashed its head against a stone block.

During her eighth pregnancy, Devaki and Vasudeva had a vision of Lord Vishnu. The Lord told them that as soon as the eighth child was born, Vasudeva should take him to the village of Vrindavan, where Yashoda, wife of the village chieftain Nandagopa, would have just delivered a baby girl. There Vasudeva was to leave his son with Yashoda and Nandagopa, and bring their daughter back to Devaki. When Sri Krishna was born as the eighth child of Devaki, Vasudeva followed the Lord Vishnu's instructions to the letter.

When the news reached Kamsa that another child had been born to Devaki, the evil king rushed to the prison cell where the baby had been born. Taking the child from Devaki's arms, he grasped it by the feet and prepared to dash its head against a rock. Unbeknownst to Kamsa, the child whose feet he was holding was actually Yogamaya, an incarnation of the Divine Mother. The goddess easily wriggled out of his grip and began to grow in size. Standing in the sky above him, Yogamaya told Kamsa, "You cannot kill me. If I wanted to I could easily kill you, but the one who is destined to slay you is alive and well and out of your reach. Your fate is sealed."

Some scholars have another theory explaining the reason Yogamaya spared Kamsa's life. The Divine Mother is so compassionate, these scholars suggest, that she will protect anyone who seeks refuge in her; traditionally, touching the feet is an expression of surrender. Even though Kamsa touched Yogamaya's feet only with the intention of killing her, her heart overflowed with compassion for him, and she spared his life.

Just like Yogamaya in the story, *mahatmas*[5] like Amma always give positive output, no matter what the input might be. For Amma, the mind is just an instrument that is completely under her control and never breaks down or malfunctions. I remember

---

[5] Literally, "great soul." Though the term is now used more broadly, in this book mahatma refers to one who abides in the knowledge that he or she is one with the Universal Self, or Atman.

one couple who would often bring their marital problems to Amma. In fact the husband had a very short temper and always blamed his wife for their problems, but every time he complained to Amma about his wife's shortcomings, Amma would staunchly defend the woman. One day the man lost his temper, this time not toward his wife but toward Amma. He raised his voice and complained that Amma never listened to his point of view, which he then proceeded to once again explain insistently. Amma listened without reacting at all. When he finally sputtered into silence and slumped down next to her chair, Amma commented serenely, "So you have worn yourself out... at least now you won't get angry at your wife today. Son, whenever you feel angry, please come and take it out on me instead of directing it toward your wife. It doesn't bother Amma at all, but your wife will take your words to heart and suffer long-lasting wounds and may even put an end to her life." Ashamed of his outburst and fearful of the potential consequences, the man apologized to Amma and later on to his wife as well. After this incident, I heard that he has mellowed considerably and is generally much more patient toward his wife.

Inspired by her example, many of Amma's devotees have been able to adjust their attitudes and thought patterns and respond more favorably to negative situations. Two of the most remarkable examples come from Gujarat. There is a Gujarati devotee whose daughter is now living at Amritapuri. Before the devastating earthquake struck Gujarat in 2001, he had been living in Ahmedabad with his wife and two children. Tragically, his wife and son lost their lives in the disaster. In the blink of an eye, he lost almost everything. Rather than being overcome with despair and losing faith in God, however, he traveled to Amritapuri and sought Amma's guidance. During the two-day train ride from Gujarat, he did not share his woes with his fellow passengers but instead talked to them about Amma's life and teachings, and even signed up twenty new subscribers for Amma's monthly spiritual magazine. The man and his daughter arrived in Amritapuri in the evening, just after Amma had returned to her room after the evening *bhajan* (devotional singing). When she heard that they had arrived, Amma called them to her room immediately. Once in the room, Amma placed their heads on her lap. Her face reflected the deep sorrow of husband and father, daughter and sister. Tears streamed down Amma's cheeks. Finally the man asked, "Amma, what should we do now?"

"Amma feels that it's better for both of you to stay at the ashram for some time," she said. "The ashram will take care of your daughter's higher studies."

Hearing this, his face brightened and he exclaimed, "Amma, we are really blessed!"

Though he mourned for his wife and son, he did not crumble under the weight of the tragedy. He was also clearly concerned about the well-being of his young daughter, and he was grateful for the opportunity to recover from his loss through service and spiritual practice.

Amma's conversation with the residents of the villages she adopted in Gujarat after the earthquake is now famous among Amma's devotees, for she often quotes their words as an example of remarkable surrender and faith in God. When Amma asked them how they were faring after the disaster, they responded, "We are fine. What God gave us, He has taken away. But we are glad that Amma is with us now."

In 2001, when the earthquake devastated parts of Gujarat, Amma responded much the same way she did to the tsunami nearly four years later—she immediately sent doctors, ambulances, brahmacharis and devotees to help. One year after the disaster, the ashram had entirely reconstructed three whole villages—a total of 1,200 houses, plus schools, community halls, water tanks, medical clinics, and roads, as well as providing electricity and sewage systems—in the area called Bhuj, where the quake's epicenter had been, and where the damage was the worst.

When the *sarpanch* (village chief) of one of Amma's adopted villages heard that Amma's own village had been hit by the tsunami, he and nine other Gujarati villagers took a train south to Amritapuri to offer their help.

"When things were bad for us, Amma came and built villages," said the sarpanch. "Now things are bad for Amma's village, so it is our dharma to help." Such is the mindset of the people of Bhuj.

One long-time devotee of Amma who spends most of his time at Amritapuri had returned to his home country to attend to some urgent family matters and was not in Amritapuri at the time of the tsunami. He anxiously followed the events as they unfolded by reading the daily reports from the ashram's website. However, after returning to India he shared that he felt a deep sense of anguish over not having been able to do more to personally help repair the damage to the ashram and serve the victims of the tsunami. As it happened, the next time he went home, a war broke out, and his country was devastated. This devotee had actually been scheduled to return to Amritapuri in the first days of the war. But after helping most of his relatives escape to safer nations, he asked Amma's blessing to stay in his country and serve the wounded and the displaced. As he moved through the war-torn streets, he found time to drop us an email. "This is my tsunami," he wrote. "I could have fled like many others in the last few days, but remembering Amma's example, my heart cannot be but deeply moved by the pain and suffering of all these distressed families. Each time I meet someone in distress, I think of Amma's smile and do whatever I can to give them some comfort and happiness."

It is a fact of life in all times and places, but especially in this day and age that we cannot expect to encounter only happy people and peaceful situations. Even when the objects of our attention are unpleasant or painful, if the subject of our mind is in good condition, we can avoid being overcome by despair, anger or depression, and our output will be beneficial to all those we meet. With a mind steeped in spiritual principles and strengthened by spiritual practice, instead of reacting automatically and often negatively to the input we receive, we can always respond in a positive way. ❖

CHAPTER 3

Here Comes a Human Being: Making the Most of Life on Earth

Only the wisest and stupidest of men never change.

—Confucius

Throughout our life, we undergo many experiences, learn many things, and perform many actions. As human beings, then, we all have multiple personalities—there is the experiencer personality, the knower personality and the doer personality. Or it can be said that our personality has these three distinct aspects.

From the moment we are born, we start experiencing the world through our senses. The faculty that enables us to make contact with both the pleasant and unpleasant in the world around us is the experiencer aspect of our personality, and it manifests from the very first moment of our life in the world.

The knower aspect of our personality is what enables us to gain knowledge. We are all endowed with the instruments of comprehension by which we can learn from the world.

The third aspect of our personality, known as the doer or performer of actions, starts later in life. As a baby, we do not deliberately plan or perform actions. We may, of course, scream and cry and make a mess in our diapers, but these are not well-planned courses of action with a definite motive. Rather, these actions are instinctive. Only later do we start performing deliberate actions.

All three aspects of our personality have a vast field of activity open to them; the possibilities for experience, knowledge and action are infinite. Unfortunately, our life span is so short that we cannot experience much, learn much or do much.

Given the limited amount of time available to us, we are faced with a choice. Which aspect of our personality will we give priority to? If we go by instinct alone, we will certainly put our emphasis on experience, and the knower and doer aspects of our personality will become the servants of the experiencer.

Even when we are in school, when we should be focused on learning, our over-emphasis on having pleasurable experiences is already obvious. For instance, most of us give primary importance to the courses that will help us make as much money as possible. This tendency continues throughout our life.

Once a man went to a bookstore in search of a book called *How to Become a Billionaire Overnight.* The sales clerk handed the man two books. The man said, "Actually, one copy will be enough."

The clerk said, "I gave you only one copy of *How to Become a Billionaire Overnight.* But when someone asks for this book, we always give another book along with it—it's a package deal."

Suddenly the customer was very interested. "Oh, really? What's the second book?"

The clerk answered, "It's a copy of the penal code."

Like this, if we focus entirely on having pleasurable experiences without gaining knowledge and engaging in right action, we can end up in trouble.

Recently I heard a story that tragically illustrates the over-emphasis we place on experience in today's world. A mountain climber who was on his way down from the summit of Mount Everest died due to lack of oxygen and frostbite. The saddest part of this tale is that Everest is not the desolate no-man's-land it was in 1953 when Sir Edmund Hillary was the first to scale its peak. With the advent of new technology and the ready availability of experienced guides, Everest has become something of a tourist attraction, albeit a costly and treacherous one. Forty people passed by the dying man on their way up the slope; any one of them could have sacrificed their chance to reach the summit in order to try to save the dying man's life by giving him oxygen and helping him down the mountain. None of them did. Each one was entirely focused on experiencing the thrill of reaching the mountain's summit and not on what they could do for another human being in desperate need of assistance.

In fact, if we give priority to the experiencer aspect of our personality, we are not much different than animals. There is only one aspect of an animal's personality, and that is the experiencer. A donkey or a chimpanzee does not go to college or come to a satsang because the knower personality is absent. A cow cannot plot a daring escape from the farm because it does not have a doer personality. Whatever action an animal does is governed by its instincts. It is this experiencer personality that we share in common with the animals. Even if we become the best experiencer in the world, with the most varied and pleasurable experiences, it is not a great achievement for a human being—it's just like competing with the animals. Maybe that's why the competition for worldly success is called the "rat race." The trouble with the rat race is that even if you win, you're still a rat.

There was an *avadhuta*[6] in Tamil Nadu who used to wander around stark naked. Whenever people passed by him, he would comment loudly, "There goes a dog!" or "There goes a donkey!" He would make these observations depending upon the *vasanas*

---

[6] Saint whose behavior does not conform to social norms.

(latent tendencies) predominant in each passerby. One day a mahatma named Ramalinga Swami happened to pass this avadhuta on the road. As soon as the avadhuta saw Ramalinga Swami approaching, he cried, "Here comes a human being!" So saying, he grabbed a cloth that was lying on the ground nearby and wrapped it around his waist. The avadhuta considered all human beings who did not have humane qualities like love, compassion or kindness as mere animals; in their presence he did not feel any need to wear clothes. But he saw Ramalinga Swami, who had realized his oneness with all of creation, as a true human being. Only in such a true master's presence did he feel ashamed of his nakedness. History proved the avadhuta correct; at the end of his life Ramalinga Swami did not leave a corpse behind but disappeared into a divine, brilliant light.

I have heard a beautiful story about a world-renowned violinist giving a concert in New York City. Having contracted polio in his youth, the musician wears leg braces and walks with crutches. That evening, as usual, the audience sat quietly while he made his way precariously across the stage to his chair, laboriously undid the clasps on his legs and picked up the violin. Finally, he nodded to the conductor, and the symphony began.

But this time, something went wrong. Midway through the performance, one of the strings on his violin broke. Everyone in the audience braced themselves for another extended delay. But the violinist merely paused, closed his eyes and then signaled the conductor to begin again.

The orchestra began, and he played from where he had left off. Though one would think that a symphonic work would sound hideous played on just three strings, the maestro managed to reinvent the piece as he went along without hitting a single disharmonious note. It was not the same, but it was good—some thought it was even better than the original.

When he finished, the audience gave him a standing ovation. When the crowd had quieted down, the musician smiled and said softly, "You know, sometimes I think it is the artist's task to find out how much music you can still make with what you have left."

If the musician had been focusing on his own experience, he would have definitely been frustrated by this further setback—a broken string on top of his broken limbs. But instead, he focused on what he had learned, and what he could still do, and he produced something more beautiful—by virtue of its obvious difficulty, if nothing else—than the original work.

According to the scriptures of *Sanatana Dharma*,[7] to live as a truly successful human being, we have to make the knower or the doer aspect of our personality predominant. It is what we know and what we do that make us a good and successful human being, rather than what we experience.

Once a woman came to Amma for darshan, saying, "Amma, my hand is in constant pain, and it is making my whole life miserable."

Amma replied, "I understand, my daughter. Amma's whole body is in constant pain."

For this woman, Amma's words were a revelation—the pain in her hand had become the focus of her entire life. Whereas, Amma was in a great deal more pain, yet she clearly did not allow this fact to hinder her activity or affect her mood in any way.

If we look at the way Amma leads her life, we can see that she does not give any importance at all to her own experience. Rather, she is totally established in Supreme Knowledge and fully

---

[7] Sanatana Dharma is the original name for Hinduism. It means, "The Eternal Way of Life."

engaged in action in the service of the world. Even as a young girl, Amma never wanted to be idle. In the midst of performing all the household chores for her own family, she would still find time to visit neighboring households and help them in whatever way possible. She would pray to God, "Please give me more and more of Your work. Let me never run out of work to do in Your name."

Amma is still living according to this philosophy today. Whenever the darshan program looks like it might finish early, Amma does whatever she can to extend it, giving more time for each individual and even singing bhajans while giving darshan, sometimes keeping one person on her shoulder for an entire song. Many of the tour staff who accompany Amma on her foreign tours see how hard she is working without food or rest and don't want to add to her burden by going for darshan themselves. But on these occasions Amma even calls the approximately 150-strong tour staff for a darshan.

As for myself, when I see a big crowd for Amma's darshan, my first thought might be, "Oh, tonight is going to be a very late night; I won't be able to get much sleep before the morning program." Of course, when the crowd gets big enough, I stop thinking about myself and start worrying about Amma. But Amma doesn't worry at all.

On Amma's 2006 North Indian Tour, some of the crowds were simply gigantic—running into the hundreds of thousands. Seeing such a crowd and realizing that Amma would embrace each one of them who had the patience to wait, one could only feel fear. If we were in her shoes, we would have run from the stage into the nearest getaway car. And if Amma had put any emphasis on the experiencer aspect of her personality, she would certainly have had a similar reaction. But Amma expressed only happiness at seeing so many of her children gathered in one place.

When Amma plans her tour schedule, she never factors in any time for rest. After the strenuous, two-month tour of North America, the swamis always ask Amma to take one or two days' rest somewhere before returning to the ashram in India. But Amma always wants to leave the very next day, saying that her children in India are waiting for her. This again shows that she doesn't give any importance to her own comforts.

Of course, Amma doesn't say that we should not enjoy pleasures, but only that they should be based on dharma. What we want for ourselves should not be harmful to others. We can earn wealth and fulfill our desires, but through righteous means. The *Taittiriya Upanishad* (1.11.1) says, "Never overlook your welfare—never neglect your prosperity." The Vedas contain many rituals which, when performed correctly, will help us to achieve our desires.[8] In fact the scriptures encourage us to be prosperous, not for the purpose of self-aggrandizement but so that we have the freedom to share our wealth with the poor and needy.

Forcing the experiencer aspect of our personality to abide by dharma will necessarily entail sacrifice and discipline; this will purify our mind to a great extent. This in turn allows us to remain calm and peaceful in the face of both pleasant and unpleasant experiences.

Once, during the American Civil War, some preachers from the North came to encourage Abraham Lincoln in his war on

---

[8] The Vedas are divided into two parts, the *Karma Kanda* (Ritual Portion) and the *Jnana Kanda* (Knowledge Portion). The Karma Kanda contains rituals designed to help one fulfill one's desires while simultaneously kindling within one an interest in spirituality. The Jnana Kanda focuses exclusively on the knowledge of Brahman, the Supreme Truth.

slavery. "Mr. President," they asked him, "Don't you think that God is on our side?"

Lincoln replied, "It doesn't concern me if God is on our side. What concerns me is whether I am on God's side."

To be on God's side means to act in accordance with dharma. Because Amma is established in the knowledge of her oneness with Brahman, she always adheres strictly to dharma, even under the most trying of circumstances. Though the ashram was badly damaged in the 2004 Asian tsunami and suffered great financial and material losses, Amma's first concern was not for the ashram at all. If not for Amma, the ashramites might well have been overwhelmed by the damage and destruction—they might have reacted, rather than responded to the devastation. But Amma's response was immediate, spontaneous and perfect. Without ever having received any training in disaster- or crisis management, Amma showed herself to be a master of the subject. As soon as the waters rushed into the ashram, her first priority was bringing the villagers to safety on the mainland.[9] After that, she turned her attention to the devotees, then to the ashramites, then to the animals residing at the ashram, and last of all to herself. Rather than retreating to a safe place, Amma was the very last to leave the affected area, ensuring first that everyone else had been transported safely to the mainland.

If we are in an accident, we will pay most attention to the part of our own body that is most injured. Likewise, seeing her Self equally in all beings, Amma's concern was for the welfare of those who had suffered the most losses. And while Amma shed many tears in the days that followed, they were not for the losses sustained by the ashram but simply in order to share the pain and

---

[9] The ashram is situated on a narrow peninsula between the Kayamkulam Backwaters and the Arabian Sea.

suffering of the villagers affected by the tragedy. The scriptures say, "When you help others, in truth you are helping yourself." When the knower aspect of our personality is fully developed, we will be able to clearly perceive this Truth—the same Self is present in everyone and in all of creation—and our every action will be for the good of the whole world.

Initially it may be difficult to see our own Self in each and every person. But if we consider each person as Amma's child or a child of God, it will be easy to see all human beings as our brothers and sisters in one worldwide family. Amma says, "For a babysitter, taking care of a baby may be a tiresome job, but for the mother, it is a joy." If we can adopt this attitude and see everyone as our own, our every action will become its own reward, and we can bring light into the lives of all those we meet. And it is not only others who will benefit; Amma says, "When we give the gift of flowers, it is we who are the first to enjoy their fragrance." Likewise, when we sacrifice our own preferences to give happiness to others, we experience a much deeper happiness and peace than we might have gained from fulfilling our own selfish desires. This is no mere platitude; there is a fundamental principle of spiritual science at work. Such actions increase our mental purity, which allows our mind to better reflect the inherent bliss of the Self. ❖

CHAPTER 4

Focusing on the Self

yasya brahmani ramate cittaṁ
nandati nandati nandatyeva

One whose mind is fixed on Brahman (the Sureme Conscious-
ness): he is blissful, he is blissful, he is only blissful.

—Bhaja Govindam, Verse 19

There is a story about a mahatma who was given an extremely precious emerald by one of his devotees. Word quickly spread that the mahatma had acquired this most coveted jewel, and before long a villager approached the mahatma and asked him to help solve his financial problems. To the villager's utter surprise, the mahatma handed over the precious emerald without the slightest hesitation. The villager went home overjoyed. However, the same villager returned to the mahatma the very next day, looking haggard and worn. After prostrating to the mahatma, the villager handed the precious jewel back to him. "What's the problem?" the mahatma asked.

"Last night I could not sleep even a wink," the villager explained. "I started thinking, 'If the mahatma is ready to give away such a valuable jewel at a moment's notice, he must have something else of even greater value.' The villager continued, "O Great One, please give me that treasure that allowed you to give away this jewel so easily."

"Are you really interested?" the mahatma asked. "Are you willing to obtain this treasure at any cost?"

When the villager responded affirmatively, the mahatma accepted him as a disciple and began to teach him about the spiritual truths.

If we are really interested in the priceless wealth of spiritual knowledge, Amma is ready to give it to us. Unfortunately, most of us are not committed to finding this hidden treasure. Rather, we are focused on acquiring the cheap trinkets of instant gratification readily available in the world around us. Amma often gives the example of offering a child the choice between a bowl of chocolates and a bowl of gold coins. The child will always choose the chocolate, not knowing that he could use the gold coins to purchase any amount of chocolate and much more as well.

There is a saying in the Hindu scriptures: "One who forsakes the Permanent in pursuit of the transient loses the Permanent; neither does the transient remain with him." If we spend all our time in pursuit of name, fame and wealth, we lose the opportunity to realize our True Self. And in the end, all that we have attained in this world—all our possessions and near and dear ones—will ultimately pass away from us. In this, we have no choice. Our only choice is whether or not to make the best use of our life to realize our true nature.

Recently a journalist asked Amma, "You have come so far in your life. You have grown from an unknown girl in an unknown village to one of the most internationally acclaimed spiritual and humanitarian leaders in the world. How do you feel when you look back on your life?"

Amma replied, "I never look back; I always look at my Self." This doesn't mean that Amma is literally looking at herself in the mirror, but that she has no regrets about the past, nor does she have any anxiety about what the future will bring, because she is always focused on the Supreme Consciousness, also known as the Atman, or Self, because it is our true nature.

When we focus on the external world, we are affected by all of the changes that take place in the world. Everything in the external world is subject to change and destruction. When we lose someone or something, or when something is changed or destroyed, we experience anger, sorrow, frustration and other negative emotions. On the other hand, our True Self is change-less. It is all-pervasive, all-powerful, and all-knowing. When our mind is fixed on this Supreme Self, we are perfectly content, and we cannot help but experience bliss.

No matter what the external circumstances, Amma is always serene and undisturbed. Most of us are quite pleasant to be around as long as things are going our way. But the moment we meet with an obstacle, we lose our peace of mind. To take a simple example, let us think about our state of mind when we reach the airport and discover that our flight has been delayed. Even if we have nothing urgent on our agenda, we become terribly restless—we can't even concentrate on CNN. We visit the ticket counter every five or ten minutes, and in between we pace back and forth, call our families, and commiserate with our fellow delayed passengers.

I heard the following story. Once, after a flight had been de-layed repeatedly, the passengers in the boarding area were tired and cranky. The airline staff tried to maintain good humor, but when the plane was finally ready, one attendant's feelings were obvi-ous. "We are now prepared to board Flight 128," he announced. "We will pre-board children traveling alone, parents with small children, and adults who are acting like children."

Amma's reaction to the same situation is very different. On her 2006 North American Tour, Amma's flights were delayed several times. However, instead of complaining or throwing up her hands in despair, Amma's reaction was very calm and cool. She used the time to practice new bhajans, inquire after the health of the devotees traveling with her, impart spiritual knowledge to her disciples, and recollect humorous incidents that took place during the darshan. On these occasions, Amma was not at all disturbed by the external circumstance of the flight delay. And the devotees traveling with her were actually grateful for it. One flight's departure was delayed by two hours. Some devotees who were on earlier flights and did not want to leave Amma in the airport were despondent. One lady even began to pray fervently that her flight would also be delayed. The next time she checked the flight status monitor, she saw that her flight, too, had been delayed indefinitely. Seeing this she began to jump for joy and ran to tell Amma the great news and thank her for the blessing.

If Amma had not been there, these very same people would surely have been as restless and disturbed as anyone else on a delayed flight and even begun demanding compensation from the airline, but because they were with Amma, it became a blissful experience for them.

There are, of course, more extreme examples wherein Amma and her tour group have met with serious adversities. But when we look into such occasions, we see that no matter how severe the difficulty, Amma is never overcome by anxiety or fear. Sixteen years ago in August 1990, when Amma visited Moscow, she gave the first evening program as scheduled in a rather austere hall. The bookstore was set up as usual, but when Amma saw the extreme poverty of the people gathered to see her, she instructed that everything in the bookstore be distributed free to the program's attendees.

Sometime during the next morning's darshan, we became aware that there were tanks rolling down the streets. When we went back to the devotee's house where Amma was staying, we learned that there had been a coup, Gorbachev was under house arrest, and the airport and main roads were closed. The government had deployed tanks at every intersection, and there was a huge ring of tanks around the Kremlin facing outward toward potential challengers.

At first, some of us traveling with Amma were very concerned, and the Russian devotees at the house came crying to Amma, overcome with fear at the possibility of a major civil war. But Amma herself was calm. She told the local devotees and those of us traveling with her not to worry, that everything would be all right.

Soon it became apparent that Amma's words had come true. The airport was opened the very next day, and very few people were injured in the attempted coup which precipitated the relatively peaceful fall of Communism. One of Amma's Russian devotees later commented, "Amma's coming symbolized the opening and healing of Russia. Her presence in Russia allowed people to cleanse their hearts, believe in themselves, and stand up for the truth."

That night, the Russian devotees informed Amma that it would not be possible to hold the public program as scheduled. Even though all of the neighboring homes were locked with the windows shuttered as the residents hid in fear for their lives, Amma asked her hosts to open up the doors of their home so that anyone who still wanted to see Amma could have the opportunity. The next day's program was held informally in the hosts' backyard. That day many Russians came to Amma for solace, guidance, and to be initiated into mantras. Even though tanks were rolling through the streets, in Amma's presence, the perils of the moment were largely forgotten.

Because Amma was not overcome by fear or distress, she was able to be there as a source of peace and guidance and provide a sanctuary for the Russian devotees in what might otherwise have been one of their darkest hours. Even amidst such turmoil, Amma was calm and content, abiding in the peace of the changeless Self.

One can better understand the concept of focusing on the Self through the metaphor of watching a movie. After watching a movie, we may feel elated, sad, bored, energized or inspired according to the events in the movie. But in reality, we didn't do anything. All the action was simply on the screen. The change in our mind was brought about not by action itself, but by our identification with the actions of the characters in the movie. Like this, our True Self is not affected by anything that happens in this world. It simply witnesses all that takes place. In actuality, we are not engaged in action. Our True Self is like the screen, rather than the characters in the movie. However, because we are identified with the body, mind and intellect, we feel elated in success and depressed in failure.

If we want to avoid being influenced by the movie, we have to constantly identify with—or pin our awareness on—the screen. Likewise, if we learn to identify with the Atman, rather than the body, mind and intellect, we can overcome the ups and downs of our life. This change in focus—from the apparent to the Real, the temporary to the Eternal—is the secret to inner peace. This is the difference between the spiritual masters and ourselves—wherever the masters look, they see only the Supreme Consciousness, or their own True Self—indivisible, perfect, complete.

Of course, no one will argue that is an easy matter to focus on the Atman, which is beyond all attributes. Amma's children often find it easier to focus on Amma and the precious memories she creates through each and every personal interaction with her devotees. As she is totally identified with the Atman, focusing on Amma is equivalent to focusing on the Self, or God. This bridge to God-consciousness is one of Amma's greatest gifts to her children.

However, focusing on the Atman does not mean just sitting in a corner with our eyes closed. After the tsunami, Amma even forbade the brahmacharis from sitting in meditation when they could be working to clear the villages of debris and later on to help construct homes for the tsunami victims. Amma says, "Real meditation means to see God, or our True Self, in all of creation." ❖

CHAPTER 5

Existence, Consciousness, Bliss

"The instant you realize God, you will be established in supreme bliss forever."

—Amma

A reporter went to interview a man on his 100th birthday. After asking a few questions about his secrets of longevity, the reporter took the old man's hand and said solemnly, "Well, sir, I hope I get the chance to wish you happy birthday next year, too."

The centenarian replied, "Why shouldn't you—you look healthy as a horse!" Despite his advanced years, the old man still refused to consider the possibility that he was going to die one day.

Irrespective of culture, gender, social status and other superficial differences, all human beings are essentially searching for three things in life. First, we want our existence to be as long as possible—some of us even look for ways to cheat death. The Pharaohs of Egypt took great pains to make sure their bodies were perfectly preserved and that they had plenty of food and even living servants to accompany them in the afterlife. Today there are those who, when faced with the prospect of their imminent demise, even entertain the possibility of being cryogenically frozen in the hopes that they can be thawed out when future scientists discover a cure for their illness and the technology to revive their body.

Beyond that, we all want to increase our knowledge. That is to say, we all want to become aware of more things, people, and places. Of course, not everyone wants to earn a PhD, but even those who are not motivated to pursue higher education will still find ways to learn more about the world, be it through travel, television, Google or neighborhood gossip.

Above all else, we want happiness. We want to be joyful all the time. It is this underlying desire that propels all of our daily actions, from the most mundane to the most ambitious, and it is only when a person has become convinced that happiness is utterly beyond reach that the prospect of an early demise becomes bearable or even appealing.

Based on these three basic life goals—longevity, knowledge, and happiness—we form many hopes and expectations, not only for ourselves but also for our loved ones. When things don't go according to our expectations, we inevitably experience sorrow. Over time, we learn that we cannot control people, places, and things nor force an outcome based on our hopes and desires.

We are all well aware of the many tragedies that have unfolded over the past couple of years. Amma has often commented, "Don't worry—life is like a tsunami." This statement may sound like cynicism or pessimism, but it is in fact just realism. What Amma means is that we should not worry about whether we will lose everything we hold dear, because in fact we definitely will. Rather than dreading this inescapable reality, if we are able to accept it as part of the natural order, we can avoid a great deal of unnecessary suffering.

In fact, the world is in a constant state of flux; nothing remains the same even for a moment. The year passes through the changing seasons, the human body passes through infancy, youth, adulthood and old age. Without constant maintenance, a road cracks and gives way to weeds and grass. Given enough time, even mountains will crumble into dust.

In *Ananda Veethi*, Amma's original composition describing her personal experience of God-realization, she proclaims, "To remove the sorrow of humanity, how many naked truths there are!"

The irrefutable fact of the imminent change and passing away of all things is evident everywhere in the world around us, but most of us turn a blind eye to this reality, stubbornly ignoring the writing on the wall.

Though we know very well the old adage, "You can't take it with you," we hoard as much money as possible even up to the moment of our death. Amma tells the following story.

Once, many patients suffering from terminal illnesses were spending their last days together in a hospice. Sensing that for some of them the end was drawing near, a nurse decided to lead them all in group prayer. She instructed them to pray with folded hands, "Dear Lord, forgive all my sins. Please accept my soul and take me in your arms…"

One among the patients didn't join his hands in prayer, keeping his fist tightly clenched instead. Before the prayer was even finished, this man slumped over and breathed his last. When he died, his clenched fist slowly opened, and there lay three coins. He had been a beggar, and he didn't join the prayer, for fear that if he opened his fist the three coins would be lost.

Of course, there is nothing wrong in earning money and ensuring that we have provided for our future, but in today's world we can see people ensuring they have enough not only for their own future, but for many generations to come. Amma says that if such people could find it in their hearts to share their good fortune with those in need, hunger and poverty could be eradicated from the face of the earth.

Ultimately, understanding the impermanence of everything in the external world will inspire us to look within. Once we realize that our primary goals of eternal life, infinite knowledge and unbroken happiness remain elusive in the external world, we begin to shift our perception, seeking these same goals internally. The scriptures of Sanatana Dharma describe our True Self as *sat-chit-ananda*, or existence, consciousness, bliss. In reality, then, the Atman is the goal that all beings seek; it is only a question of whether this seeking is done directly or indirectly.

This description of our Self is not arbitrary, nor is it blind faith. The ancient sages of India looked within and realized their own true nature. They spoke from their direct experience, and their descriptions can be verified even from our own limited state of awareness. Let us look closely at each of the three qualities attributed to the Self.

First of all, we know that we are here now, existing. We may deny the existence of God, but no one will deny their own existence. Something cannot come out of nothing; the table exists now as a table, but before that it existed as a tree, and before that it existed as a seed. The seed came from another tree. If one continues to trace these elements backward, we must finally accept that existence is fundamental; only the name and form changes. Thus we can see that *sat* (existence) is an incontrovertible aspect of our True Self.

The second aspect our Self is described as *chit* (consciousness, or knowledge). It is this consciousness that makes us aware of our own existence and all of creation. How do we know that we are consciousness? When we fall into a deep sleep, for all practical purposes, we disappear; we are dead to the world. We are unaware of having a body. We have no memory, no desires, and we seem to have no experience. However, when we wake up, we say, "Oh, I slept well." How do we know that we had a good sleep? It is because even when our body, mind, and intellect are asleep, our consciousness remains constant. In fact, pure consciousness is the only consistent element in the three states of waking, dreaming, and deep sleep. During the waking and dreaming states, consciousness is aware of objects—names and forms; while in deep sleep, consciousness is aware of their absence.

The third aspect of our Self is described as *ananda* or bliss. Given the opportunity, most people would like to sleep as much as possible. This is because during deep sleep, the mind is not functioning and we experience bliss. This indicates that our real nature, when nothing else—thoughts, feelings, desires, fears—is superimposed over it, is bliss and joy. Just as the surface of a calm lake clearly reflects the moon, when our mind becomes still and quiet—when our thoughts and desires subside—we naturally feel blissful.

In the *Brhadaranyaka Upanishad*, it is said,

na vā are patyuḥ kāmāya patiḥ priyo bhavati
ātmanastu kāmāya pati priyo bhavati

The wife loves the husband not for the sake of the husband but for her own sake (and vice versa).

(2.4.5)

This may sound like a harsh statement, but if we examine it closely, its truth becomes apparent. Everyone proclaims an undying love for family, but what happens when a family member betrays us? The husband divorces the wife, the sister becomes estranged from the brother, and the mother disowns the son. If we really loved our relatives, we would continue to love them even if they began treating us badly and no longer gave us any happiness.

Sometimes when a young man or woman joins the ashram, their parents, who had nursed high hopes of their children looking after them in their old age and ultimately of having grandchildren, naturally feel upset. Some years back the parents of a young man who had become an ashram resident came to the ashram during Amma's absence and made quite a scene. In the end the parents loudly declared that they were going on a hunger strike; until their son agreed to move back home and get married to the girl they had chosen for him, they would refuse to eat anything. This put the young man in a serious bind; he was deeply concerned for his parents' welfare. At the same time he felt that a life of service and spiritual practice was his true calling. As a compromise, without telling them about his decision, he also began fasting. As long as they did not eat, he told himself, he would not eat anything either. However, after two days, when it became apparent that the young man was not going to change his mind, his parents ate a hearty breakfast and caught the next train home. Later on, the boy paid a visit to his parents and did his best to console them and explain his point of view before returning to his life in the ashram.

If a person or object is not giving us happiness, we will not even be interested in, let alone love that person or object. This shows that we only love that which gives us happiness.

One day a man complained to the health department about his brothers. "I have six brothers," he said. "We all live in one room. They have too many pets—one has seven monkeys and another has seven dogs. It's terrible—there's no air in the room at all. You've got to do something about it."

"Have you got any windows?" asked the health department official.

"Yes," said the man.

"Why don't you open them?" the official suggested.

"What?!" the man shouted, as if it was the most preposterous suggestion he had ever heard. "And lose all my pigeons?"

Just like the man in the story, most of us are more than willing to overlook our own faults—we love ourselves unconditionally and absolutely. Thus, it follows that our Self must be a source of unconditional and absolute happiness. Even those who feel a kind of self-hatred or have suicidal thoughts do not really hate themselves; they only dislike their circumstances or mental state. If their problems were suddenly solved or their mind became peaceful, they would want to go on living. In fact, the scriptures tell us that our Self is not only *a* source but *the* source of all happiness. Even when we feel that something external is giving us happiness, it is only that we have satisfied a desire, and thus the mind is relatively quiet. Just as still waters clearly reflect the moon's image, the quieter our mind becomes, the more clearly it reflects the inherent bliss of the Self.

We usually seek whatever makes us happy in the short term. But as the saying goes, "Short-term profits make for long-term losses." In the past, we have attempted to enrich our life with so many valuable things, but they have not given us lasting happiness or peace. If they had, we would not be seeking any more; you would not be reading this book.

We already have many years of experience—whether through relationships, achievements, possessions, dwelling places or vacations—in searching for satisfaction in the outside world. One experience should be enough for us to correctly analyze a situation. If we are cooking rice and want to know if it is ready, it's enough to take only one grain. There is no need to taste each and every grain in the pot.

There is a story about two soldiers who are caught and taken as prisoners of war. One becomes reconciled with his captivity and chooses to live out his life as a slave for his enemy. The other one earnestly studies the ways and means of his escape, even while toiling as a prisoner.

Just like the prisoners in the story, we have a choice. Most people are like the first prisoner, settling for the fleeting moments of happiness they can get from the outside world, while remaining a slave to their likes and dislikes, desires and fears. Instead, we should try to be like the second prisoner—we should direct our attention inward in an effort to break free of our attachment and aversion toward the people and objects of the world. Once we make a conscious decision to turn our awareness inward, we discover that our three goals—eternal life, infinite knowledge, and unbroken happiness—have always been there within us, as our own True Self. ❖

CHAPTER 6

"Mind Change, Please!"

If the doors of perception were cleansed, everything would appear to man as it is—infinite.

—William Blake

Recently I received the following anecdote in a letter from a devotee. It was written as a joke, but it is actually quite instructive.

It started out innocently enough. I began to think at parties now and then, just to loosen up. Inevitably though, one thought led to another, and soon I was more than just a social thinker. I began to think even when I was all by myself. Thinking became more and more important to me, and finally I was thinking all the time. I just couldn't control myself—I began to think on the job. Soon I had a reputation at work as a heavy thinker. One day the boss called me in and said, "I like you, and it hurts me to say this, but your thinking has become a real problem. If you don't stop thinking on the job, we're going to have to let you go." This gave me a lot to think about.

At my next checkup, my doctor told me that my heavy thinking was giving me high blood pressure and that if I went on like this, I might not live much longer. But today, I'm a recovering thinker. Life is so much more peaceful now that I stopped thinking!

Imagine a monkey, mischievous enough when sober, who has somehow gotten himself extremely drunk. Then imagine that this same drunken monkey, in the course of his antics, is stung by a scorpion and begins to hop around, howling in pain. This drunken, scorpion-stung monkey then passes under a coconut tree and, exactly at that moment, a large green coconut drops from the tree onto his head. Finally, reeling here and there, the poor primate is possessed by a ghost. Amma says that the above scenario is a good analogy for our present state of mind, with our limited awareness immersed in likes and dislikes, desires and fears.

With such a mind, we are not able to see things as they are. Rather, we see them as we are. The following story illustrates this point.

Once there was a Zen monastery occupied by two monks. One of the monks happened to have only one eye. One day a traveling monk knocked on the door and challenged the one-eyed monk to a philosophical debate. When the contest was over, the traveling monk admitted his defeat. Before leaving, he went to take leave of the other monk, who was the head of the monastery. The visiting monk told the head monk, "That one-eyed monk is a genius. We decided to debate in silence. I went first and showed a single finger—signifying the Buddha. Your brother showed two fingers, meaning the Buddha and his teachings. I replied with three fingers, indicating the Buddha, his teachings and his followers. The one-eyed monk replied with the *coup de grâce* when he showed me his fist—proving that, in reality, the Buddha, his teachings and his followers are all one." The visiting monk bowed once more and left the monastery.

Just then the one-eyed monk entered. He was totally irate. "That monk was so rude. If he had not been our guest, I would have given him the beating he deserved."

"What happened?" asked the head monk. The one-eyed monk replied, "We decided to have a silent debate. The first thing he did was to put a single finger up meaning, 'I see you have only one eye.' So I put up two fingers out of courtesy to him, meaning, 'I see you have two eyes.' But that rascal had the nerve to put up three fingers telling me that together, the two of us have three eyes. I got so mad I shook my fist, meaning, 'If you don't stop talking about eyes, I'm going to punch your lights out.'" Based on their respective mindsets, the two monks interpreted the hand gestures totally differently.

One evening the Buddha was giving a sermon. Keeping in mind the monks who were present in the audience, at the end of the sermon he said, "Before you go to sleep, don't forget to do the most important thing of the day."

Hearing these words, the monks thought, "We must not forget to meditate before sleeping."

A thief was also present in the audience, however, and he interpreted the Buddha's words in a different way. "The Lord Buddha is right," he mused. "Late night is the best time for stealing." A prostitute hearing these words thought that she should try to get some customers that night on the way home from the sermon. Each one took the Buddha's instruction according to his or her own frame of mind.

When problems arise in our lives, Amma says that we always try to change the circumstances, but in many cases the only appropriate solution is to change ourselves—to change our mind.

During one of Amma's programs in Japan, a devotee came to one of Amma's brahmacharis and described all the problems he was having with his wife. The brahmachari listened to him patiently and finally suggested that he go for Amma's darshan with a prayer in mind that she help restore the harmony to his marriage.

When he was in her lap, Amma whispered in his ear, "My darling son, my darling son," in Japanese. But he misunderstood what Amma was saying, and instead thought she was saying the Japanese words for, "What are you going to do? What are you going to do?"

He thought, "Oh, Amma! You're giving me a choice?!" Overcome with excitement, he blurted out, in broken English, his secret desire for another wife: "Amma! Wife change, please! Wife change, please!" Amma had a hearty laugh and put his head back in her lap. After the devotee's darshan, when he realized that everyone around had heard his exclamation, he became very embarrassed.

But the next time he went for darshan, Amma said to him, "Son, mind change, please, not wife!" Hearing Amma's advice, the man realized his folly and resolved to make more efforts to adjust and get along with his wife.

Mahatmas like Amma are truly happy living in the same world as we live. Though they face the same difficult situations, they are always at peace. When Amma was a young girl, her parents would send her to do household chores—after she had completed all the work for her own family—at a relative's house nearly seven miles away. At first Amma would take a boat to reach her relative's, but as her parents began complaining about the expense, Amma decided to walk instead. Rather than spending the long walk bemoaning her fate, however, Amma would spend it listening to the sound of the waves beating against the shore, or she would chant Om silently or sing softly to the Lord. Amma says the joy she experienced during those walks was beyond words.

In his *Five Verses on Spiritual Life* (*Sadhana Panchakam*), the great sage Adi Shankaryachara admonishes us:

ekānte sukham āsyatām

Dwell happily in solitude.

The solitude mentioned here does not necessarily mean physical solitude or isolation. *Eka* means "one" and *anta* means "end," or "goal." When the mind is engaged in deep contemplation of the guru, God, or the Atman, it is focused in one direction. The mind becomes peaceful and relaxed. This is real solitude.

Of course, we can very well be alone with nobody around to disturb us, but with a mind invaded by thoughts and emotions, there can be no peace or joy.

Once there was a monastery that was very strict. Following a vow of silence, no one was allowed to speak at all; there was only one exception to this rule. Every ten years, the monks were permitted to speak just two words. After spending his first ten years at the monastery, one monk went to the head monk. "It has been ten years," said the head monk. "What are the two words you would like to speak?"

"Bed... hard..." said the monk.

"I see," replied the head monk.

Ten years later, the same monk returned to the head monk's office. "It has been ten more years," said the head monk. "What are the two words you would like to speak?"

"Food... stinks..." said the monk.

"I see," replied the head monk.

Yet another ten years passed and the monk again met with the head monk who asked, "What are your two words now?"

"I quit!" said the monk.

"Well, I can see why," replied the head monk. "All you ever do is complain."

Even in the most suitable circumstances, if our attitude is not correct, we will never find peace of mind. Yet once we have reached true solitude, even if we are in a shopping mall, our mind will stay composed. Our own mind is the cause of our suffering, and our own mind is the cause of our joy.

Once, to help generate feelings of harmony and brotherhood and to inspire the budding artists in his school, a high-school principal offered a prize to the artist who could paint the best representation of peace. After receiving and reviewing many submissions, the principal narrowed her choice down to two. One portrayed a calm lake, perfectly reflecting evergreen groves and the snowcapped mountains behind them; overhead was a blue sky dotted with soft white clouds.

The second painting had mountains, too, but these were rugged and bare. Above was depicted a dark and formidable sky, overcast by towering thunderclouds and jagged flashes of lightning. Down the side of the mountain tumbled a ferocious waterfall.

The principal called her staff in to look at the two paintings and give their opinions as to which one was the best representation of peace. Unanimously, they recommended the principal choose the first one; after all, any fool could see it was the more peaceful scene. In the end, though, the principal picked the second painting. One of the teachers asked her why.

"Look closer," the principal advised him. When he did so, he saw that behind the waterfall a tiny bush was growing out of a jagged crevice in the side of the mountain. In that bush, very close to the rushing torrent, a mother bird sat on her nest in perfect peace. "Peace does not mean to be in a place where there is no noise, trouble or hard work," the principal explained. "Peace means to be in the midst of all those things and still be calm within. That is real peace."

Gaining mastery over our mind is not just a tool for psychological well-being; according to the scriptures, it is literally a matter of life and death. Often the last thought in our mind at the time of our death plays an important role in determining our next life. In the *Bhagavad Gita*, Sri Krishna declares,

antakāle ca mām eva smaran muktvā kalevaram
yaḥ prayāti sa madbhāvaṁ yāti nā'styatra saṁśayaḥ

And whoever, at the time of death, leaving the body,
goes forth remembering Me alone, he attains My being; there
is no doubt about this.

(8.5)

Amma tells the following story.

There were two friends; one of them was very interested in spirituality, the other was indifferent. One evening, a *satsang*[10] on the *Bhagavad Gita* took place in their city. The first man wanted to attend and asked his friend to come with him. The other man was not interested. He wanted to go to a nightclub instead. Each one went his own way. After some time, the man at the satsang started thinking, "My friend must be having a good time. I should have gone with him." At the same time, the man in the nightclub was thinking: "Why did I come here? All these dances are pretty much the same; it would have been much more interesting to hear about the *Bhagavad Gita*, and at least then I could have gained some *punya* (merit)."

---

[10] Literally, "association with the Truth." The highest form of satsang is samadhi, or total absorption in the Absolute. Satsang can also mean being in the presence of a spiritual master, association with other spiritual seekers, reading spiritual books or listening to a discourse on spirituality.

It so happened that both of them died that same night. The one who had physically gone to the night club, but whose mind had been on Sri Krishna, found himself in heaven. The other one, whose mind had been in the nightclub, found himself somewhere less desirable. Without putting forth the necessary effort to gain mastery over our mind, we will not be able to make the most of our present life, and our future life may be negatively affected as well.

Once a man walked into a psychiatrist's office and said, "Doctor, please help me. I think that I am God."

"*Hmmm*, very interesting. Tell me, how did it start?"

"Well, first I created the sun, then the moon, then the earth and the stars..."

Though this man was merely suffering from delusion, ultimately the truth is that we are all God. The *Taittiriya Upanishad* (2.6.3) says, "The Supreme Being thought, 'Let me be many,' and He created all that we perceive. Having created it, He entered into it." According to Sanatana Dharma, there is only God, and nothing else.

Ultimately, Amma says, this world of apparent differences is an illusion, and if we want to realize the Supreme Truth, we have to go beyond the mind completely—for the source of the illusion is the mind itself.

En route from one city to another on one of Amma's Indian tours, as usual Amma stopped to serve lunch to the tour group. After everyone had finished eating, Amma asked an eight-year-old boy named Ramu a question: "Where is God?"

Ramu pointed up to the sky.

"No, inside," Amma said. "God is inside of you." And then pointing to the 400 or so people circled around her, "God is inside each and every one of these people here. We should serve everyone, seeing them all as embodiments of God."

Amma then asked the boy to explain his concept of God.

"God created the world and all the people," Ramu said.

"The world is not God's creation," Amma replied. "It is your creation."

Voluminous works like the *Yoga Vasishtha* have been composed in order to illumine this profound truth: the entire universe is nothing but a projection of the mind. Ramu stood perplexed. Then, staring up into Amma's eyes, he finally—without confidence—said, "Amma is joking."

Amma says that anything that we see in this world, we see through our preconceived notions. We perceive the world through the limited instruments of our mind and intellect—that is why the scriptures say that what we consider as the truth is not the absolute truth, but only a relative truth—created by our mind.

In a similar way, Amma says we consider this world to be real, but in fact it is just an illusion. Let us take the example of a clay pot. Before the pot came into being, the clay existed. And if the pot is dropped and broken into pieces, the pot as a separate entity disappears, but the clay that formed the pot is still there. Thus the pot has no existence of its own; it is nothing but clay. For a period of time the clay took the form of a pot—being of temporary nature, the pot was only relatively real. Because it has no independent existence apart from the clay, we can say that, in the ultimate sense, the pot does not exist—it is an illusion.

Likewise when Amma told the boy, "The world is the creation of your mind," she meant that the world of duality is an illusion created by our mind. In fact, there is only Brahman—there is only God. But in our present state, we see and experience so much duality in the world.

Amma says what we call the illusion of duality does not really exist—it is like darkness. We cannot remove darkness as such and place it somewhere. The only way to overcome darkness is to turn on the light. As soon as we turn on the light, darkness disappears. Likewise, when the light of Self-knowledge dawns within us, the darkness of duality disappears, and we see oneness everywhere.

In the *Isavasya Upanishad*, it is said about the Atman:

tadejati tannaijati tad dūre tadvantike
tadantarasya sarvasya tadu sarvasyāsya bāhyataḥ

That moves, That does not move;
That is far off, That is very near;
That pervades everything,
and that is beyond everything.

(5)

In fact, the Atman is nearer than the nearest—it being our very Self, it is nearer even than the mind. It is the central existence of every living being and the substratum of the entire universe; there is nothing nearer than the Atman. But it is said that the Self appears to be farther than the farthest, because it is unattainable by the ignorant even in hundreds of millions of years. This does not mean that God is cruel, however. The eternal, blissful nature of our True Self is a secret, but no one is deliberately keeping it from us, least of all God or the guru. It is only that we lack the subtlety of mind to properly understand it. To those whose minds are clouded by the ego, this knowledge is as though hidden, in the same way that a melody is hidden from a tone-deaf person or certain colors are hidden from the color-blind. It remains hidden until a suitable person appears to receive the teaching. Amma says she is just waiting for such recipients to appear. Let's not make her wait any longer. ❧

CHAPTER 7

Senses and Sensibility: How to Restrain the Mind and Look Within

I have discovered that all human evil comes from this:man's being unable to sit still in a room.

—Blaise Pascal

In his *Crest-Jewel of Discrimination* (*Viveka Chudamani*), Shankaracharya declares:

doṣeṇa tīvro viṣayaḥ kṛṣṇa-sarpa-viṣād api
viṣaṁ nihanti bhoktāraṁ draṣṭāraṁ cakṣuṣā'pyayam

Sense objects are more deadly than the poison of the king cobra.
The cobra's poison is fatal only when taken,
but these—on mere sight—can cause death.

(77)

The king cobra's venom is lethal—one bite from this snake and we have just half an hour to live. However, it is said that the sense objects are even more dangerous; while the cobra has to bite us in order to kill us, just looking at a sense object is enough to destroy us. Seeing something desirable, we want to acquire it, and in the headlong attempt to make it our own, we go astray from the path of dharma. Amma illustrates this truth with the following story.

73

Once, an avadhuta was walking toward his village. At the side of the road there was a huge tree with a hole in the trunk. He decided to rest a little in the shade of the tree. After his nap, as he was about to continue on his way, he looked in the trunk of the tree. When he saw what was hidden therein, he jumped as if he had been given a jolt and ran off, shouting, "Danger! Danger! I saw Yama, the Lord of Death, in that tree. Run for your lives!" Just then, three men were passing by, and they asked the avadhuta what had happened to him. He explained that Yama was waiting for them in the tree and warned that they should not go near it. Of course, when someone tells us not to do something, we suddenly feel like doing it—such is human nature. The three men decided to go and see for themselves, thinking the avadhuta might be a little crazy and wondering what he had actually seen.

When they looked into the hole in the tree's trunk, they saw a treasure of diamonds and other glittering gems. "What an idiot," one of the men exclaimed. "He saw the treasure and thought it was the Lord of Death. The fool has fled. What luck for us!"

The tree being by the side of a busy thoroughfare, many people were passing by. So the three accomplices chose one among them—call him A—to watch the treasure and let them know as soon as nobody was around, so that they could divide the booty three ways. The other two, B and C, secretly devised a plan of their own. They agreed to kill A so that they would only have to divide the treasure into two. As it was getting late, they started feeling hungry. B offered to go and find food. On the way, he went to A and told him that C was a gangster ready to kill him. A answered, "Let him try! I will teach him a lesson!"

B went to get the food but on the way back, he mixed poison with it, so that he could kill the others and keep the treasure for himself. When he brought the food to A, the latter killed him by

74

surprise. Then A took the food and went to the tree to eat with C, and both of them died. Some time later the avadhuta happened to pass by again and saw the three corpses. He called out again, "The Lord of Death is around—keep clear!"

The mere sight of the jewels led these three men to death. How many deaths have been incurred by the thirst for material possessions? It is in this sense that Shankaracharya says that the sense objects are even more lethal than snake venom.

This does not mean that the sense organs are our enemies; they are only mediums through which the mind enjoys the sense objects. The eyes do not relish the sight of anything; they simply relay information to the mind. In fact, without the mind's participation, the sense organs do not register anything at all. How often have we been engrossed in a book or a TV program and failed to hear someone talking right next to us? The real culprit is the mind and not the sense organs. If we can restrain the mind, the sense organs will leave us in peace.

The first step in restraining the mind is to make an effort to stay away from the objects and situations that we know will tempt us to indulge in them. Amma says it will be difficult to give up chocolate if we walk around with chocolates in our handbag, or stop watching television if we have a plasma TV on our bedroom wall.

However, even if we physically cut ourselves off from the object of our desire, if we continue thinking about the desired object, it will not be of much benefit. If, for instance, we are meditating and the smell of delicious food comes to our nostrils, our mind will go to the kitchen, and we will wonder what delicacy is being prepared. We cannot physically get up and go to the kitchen because we are supposed to be meditating. So our body remains in the meditation hall, but our mind is in the kitchen; our body is fasting, but our mind is having a feast. In the *Bhagavad Gita*, Sri Krishna says,

> *karmendriyāṇi saṁyamya*
> *ya āste manasā smaran*
> *indriyārthān vimūḍhātmā*
> *mithyācāraḥ sa ucyate*
>
> *One who masters the organs of action*
> *but whose mind is still attached to the sense objects cradles*
> *illusions;*
> *he is called a hypocrite.*

(3.6)

Our mind can be compared to a pot of water placed over a fire. When the water boils, we add a little cold water to cool it down. It works for a short time; then again the water boils, and again we pour in cold water. If we want to avoid having to add cold water every two minutes, we should pour water on the fire itself. Likewise, our mind boils because of the fire of our desires. When a desire is satisfied, the mind cools down—it is at peace for a while—but before long another desire arises, and it boils anew. Desires have no end; there is always another one, and then another. The only solution is to pour the water of spiritual understanding over the fire of our desires. Even if we don't succeed in putting out the fire, we can certainly reduce the intensity of the flames. When we understand that indulging the senses is counterproductive—in that it leads us away from our True Self—we will not let ourselves be swayed by temptation.

In the *Bhagavad Gita* (18.37, 38), Sri Krishna explains, "What seems at first like nectar leads to poison; what seems at first like poison leads to nectar." When our senses make contact with the objects of our desire, we enjoy them in the moment, but these pleasures later end in sorrow when the objects naturally change or diminish. On the other hand, true peace and happiness, acquired through restraint of the mind, renunciation of desire and spiritual practice has a bitter beginning-insofar as it is difficult to discipline the mind. However, we soon find that the happiness to be found in the world pales in comparison to the inner peace arising from regular spiritual practice, let alone the boundless bliss of Self-realization.

After the fire has burned down, we can easily take the pot away from the fire. In the same way, after our mind is relatively free of desire, it will be easier to withdraw our attention from the sense organs and turn inward—toward the Atman. ❖

CHAPTER 8

Transcending Desire

By three methods we may learn wisdom: First, by reflection, which is noblest; Second, by imitation, which is easiest; and third by experience, which is the bitterest.

—Confucius

Recently, I saw the son of an American devotee reading a book about the human body. Giving him a pop quiz, I asked him, "What makes up seventy percent of your body?" Without missing a beat, the boy answered, "Coca-Cola."

Actually, there are two types of desires: natural and cultivated. If we are thirsty, it is a natural desire. But if we want to drink only soda, it is a cultivated desire. Leading a spiritual life means discriminating between natural desires and cultivated desires, and transcending the cultivated ones. If they can be eliminated, we can save a great deal energy, effort and time that can be used for spiritual practice, in service of society or for any other creative purpose.

Shortly after Amma announced the details of her massive tsunami relief effort, an Australian couple who had met Amma on her previous visit to Australia was in the car on their way to an expensive restaurant to celebrate their wedding anniversary. Suddenly the woman spoke up. "Sweetheart, how much do you think tonight's dinner will cost?"

"Don't think about that, darling," her husband replied. "On our anniversary, money is no object."

"Because I was just thinking," the wife continued. "We could easily spend $200 on dinner tonight. What if we turn around and have dinner at home? We could order in for less than twenty dollars, and the remaining money we could send to Amma for the tsunami victims."

Her husband did as she suggested, and, knowing that their small sacrifice would help Amma serve the truly needy, they both enjoyed their simple Chinese takeout more than any anniversary dinner they had ever had. In fact, the husband was so inspired by his wife's idea that he told all his coworkers about it the next day. By week's end, he was able to send a check comprising not only the money he and his wife had saved by eating dinner at home that night, but also generous donations from many of his coworkers as well. They had all decided to make a similar sacrifice for their wedding anniversaries that year.

The easiest way to transcend our cultivated desires is to approach a true master like Amma. I don't mean that if you come to Amma, all of your desires will disappear immediately. But it is the experience of many of Amma's devotees and disciples that when we met Amma, many of our desires simply fell away. I came to Amma hoping her divine power would be enough to secure me a transfer to a bank closer to my hometown. The main reason I wanted a transfer was that I was very dissatisfied with the accommodation and food available to me in the town where I was working at that time. After meeting Amma, I started spending most of my time at the ashram, despite the fact that there was no accommodation and very limited food. In Amma's presence, what had been of primary importance to me spontaneously faded into the background.

One young man who had cherished the dream of working as a flight attendant suddenly found himself with job offers from two different airlines. Unable to choose between the two, he decided to get Amma's opinion. But when he received Amma's darshan, he didn't even ask the question, deciding instead to keep his old job in his hometown, which was situated near the ashram and would give him plenty of opportunities to see Amma and participate in the ashram's spiritual and service activities. Just like that, his lifelong desire to fly fell away—he was aiming for something even higher.

This is a strange but common phenomenon—many of us come to Amma with hundreds of problems, thinking, "If I tell these problems to Amma, by her grace, they might be solved." But when we come near Amma, we can't even articulate a word—we forget everything. In Amma's presence, we are filled with the love and peace that she constantly radiates. Her divine vibrations replenish and calm us. The joy we experience in Amma's presence is a kind of preview—it is a tiny glimpse of the eternal bliss that lies within us, and which we can attain by realizing our oneness with God.

Of course, when we leave Amma's presence, our desires and problems resurge, and we find ourselves agitated again. But we can learn from the experience we have had in Amma's presence. She shows us that when the mind is freed from all thoughts and desires, only peace and bliss remain—we see to the core of our being, which is nothing other than the Atman, or God. The taste of bliss we receive in Amma's presence enables us to see that the happiness we feel when we abandon desires is much greater than what we derive from satisfying those same desires.

In fact, satisfying a desire is merely the process of eliminating the desire. For instance, if we want a sports car, we buy it and the desire for a sports car disappears. By purchasing the sports car, we eliminated the desire for it. By the same token, if we simply eliminate our cultivated desires—through discrimination, by spending time in the presence of a spiritual master, or by substituting the desire for something higher in its place—we don't have to go to all the trouble of fulfilling them, and so much time and energy is saved. It is also worth remembering that there are a great many desires we would not be able to fulfill even if we tried.

Of course, there are surely basic desires and necessities—these can be considered as natural desires. Depending on our lifestyle, we may need a car; as spiritual aspirants, it is the cultivated desire for a sports car that we want to eliminate. If our goal is God-realization, it is better to stay away from that which is dispensable.

During Amma's most recent North Indian Tour, Amma stopped for lunch in a field on top of a small hill. The devotees traveling with her gathered around, and a Western devotee came forth with a question. "Amma, when we are facing a very strong attachment—something we are so identified with that we can't get rid of it—what is the proper attitude?"

Amma replied, "If your desire is intense and you try to suppress it, it will only return with more power. On the other hand, even after we have the experience once or twice or three times, the desire will still keep coming back, so we shouldn't think that it will be satiated through indulging."

Giving the example of the desire for partnership, Amma said, "Even at the age of 100, it will not go, and even if one gets married, he or she may still become attracted to other people. At some point we must try to cultivate *vairagya* (dispassion)."

The man was not satisfied with Amma's answer. In fact, he had a very specific desire in his mind. "Amma, I want to sail my boat from America to India… this is a plan that I've had for many years."

Amma asked him how long it would take to sail from America to India.

"Between two months and 10 years."

The peaceful hillside erupted in laughter.

"Has someone done this before?" Amma asked him. "It's not like just going on a ship; many factors are involved."

The man told Amma that, yes, many people had made similar voyages, adding that he had been living on the sea for the past twenty years.

"Even after being on the sea for twenty years, this desire has not been exhausted," Amma pointed out. "So maybe you can pray to God, 'In the next life make me a dolphin!'"

Again came the laughter, but the man protested. "The point is to get rid of the vasana. That's what I want."

Seeing his earnest desire for help, Amma's compassion flowed forth: "No. By fulfilling a vasana, it can never be exhausted. The dispassion that results is only *smashana vairagya* (the temporary dispassion that arises when we visit a cremation ground)—when one's beloved wife dies, he may say, 'I am never going to remarry,' but after some time he marries again."

Amma then told the man that if he properly studied the route and all the potential problems and if his desire was still really strong, then he could make the trip. But Amma did wonder what he thought was so special about the voyage. She asked him as much, and he confessed that, in fact, he did not know.

Amma then told him that during the journey he should constantly watch his mind and reflect. She told him to break the trip into legs, and to do one section and see how his mind was reacting. Similarly, the second leg and third leg. "Each time you finish one leg, watch the mind. See if the desire to continue still persists. If you want to continue, go ahead. But after you've finished the third leg, if the desire still remains, you should realize that it is never going to go. At that point, please stop."

To conclude, Amma made perhaps the most penetrating comment of the afternoon: "The effort you are putting forth for the voyage could be better utilized for helping the poor—buying them food and clothing and looking after their education. Look and see if your desire to sail isn't just the naughtiness of the mind."

Amma's advice to this troubled sailor applies just as well to our own desires. We can never exhaust them through indulgence, and if we suppress them, they will bounce back like a tightly coiled spring. Instead of mere repression of our desires, we should substitute noble ideas and actions in their place, and the desires will fall away of their own accord.

There is a beautiful story in the epic Puranas. One day Kubera, the god of wealth and a devotee of Lord Shiva, thought to himself, "The Lord has taken the appearance of a beggar. As the people of the world are becoming more selfish every day, how much can the Lord possibly collect in alms, with which he has to look after the entire world? As the Lord will put the world before his own family, his son Ganesha may not be getting enough to eat." Thinking thus, Kubera invited Lord Ganesha for a grand feast. Ganesha arrived at Kubera's palace and saw an enormous meal laid out before him. Kubera instructed him, "My dear Ganesha, please take as much as you want—eat to your fill." Before Kubera knew it, Ganesha had devoured the entire meal; there was nothing left. Still hungry, Ganesha started eating the plates, spoons and knives, even the table. When he had finished devouring everything in the entire room, he looked over at Kubera. There was something about the way Ganesha was looking at him that suddenly made him feel afraid. Kubera took to his heels, but Ganesha chased after him. Running as fast as he could, he eventually sought refuge in Ganesha's father, Lord Shiva. Actually, he hid behind Lord Shiva himself. Ganesha charged straight forward to where they were standing. At the last minute, Shiva extended his arm, holding out in the open palm of his hand just one grain of puffed rice. Ganesha stopped in his tracks, picked up the solitary grain with his trunk, and put it in his mouth. Instantly, his hunger subsided.

Though we may feel it to be the curse of our existence, in truth, our discontentment—the persistent feeling of incompleteness—is in fact a precious gift from God. If, with a pure mind, we honestly inquire, we will see that all our wants—and the blows and frustrations and sorrows we face in pursuing their fulfillment—are pointing us toward God. As the 17th century Christian monk Jean Pierre de Caussade wrote: "God instructs the heart not with ideas...but through pain and contradictions."

In fact, Ganesha represents each one of us, and the king's feast represents all the experiences and pleasurable things of the world. The story is teaching us that the lack we feel within—the dissatisfaction, the restlessness—will never be satisfied by the things of the world. Lord Shiva represents the guru whose single word, glance or touch can offer us complete fulfillment.[11] Just as puffed rice cannot sprout, so too the guru's teachings and grace bring an end to the cycle of birth and death. Only when, guided by the guru, we realize our oneness with God will our hunger finally be appeased and will we know true peace and contentment. ❖

---

[11] Lord Shiva is considered the primordial guru.

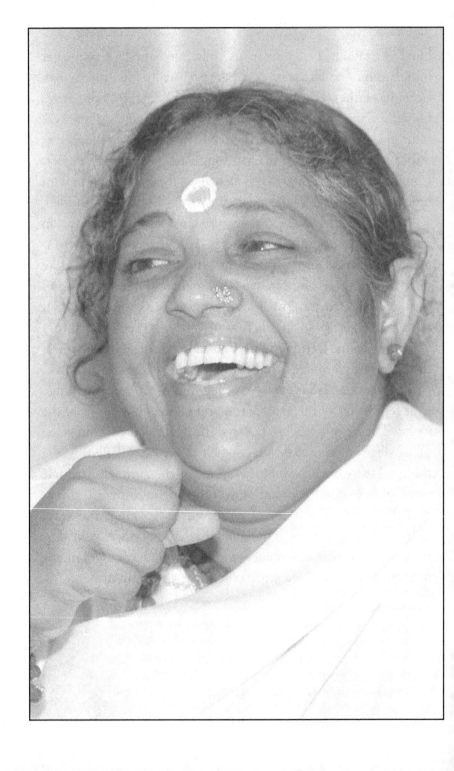

CHAPTER 9

Life after Death

"Death is not the end; it is just like the period at the end of a sentence. It is the beginning of a new life."

—Amma

Some years ago a Western woman came with her two small children to live at Amma's ashram in India. The children were naturally attracted to Amma and became very attached to her, even spending hours every day with Amma in her room after the day's darshan was finished. One of the boys in particular had a very close connection to Amma, and she used to gaze lovingly into his eyes for what seemed like ages. The boy never shied away from Amma or even blinked while she was looking at him. Through the son, the mother also became very attached to Amma. However, after they had stayed in the ashram for a few years, due to some family problems, it seemed they would have to leave the ashram at least for a few months. Amma advised the distraught mother to sort out the problems and return as soon as she could, but the mother was inconsolable. She had become so attached to Amma and to the ashram that she was unable to bear the thought of leaving, even for a short time.

In time, it became apparent that at least a brief sojourn to her home country was unavoidable. So the mother and her two boys booked a flight home, promising to return as soon as possible. A couple of days after their departure, we received the tragic news that the very same day they had arrived in their home country, the boys' mother had had a heart attack and died instantly. Amma was informed during the morning darshan. She shed tears throughout the remainder of the darshan and intermittently in the days to come as well. Whenever she was seen crying, she always spoke of the terrible anguish the two boys must be experiencing. Even though Amma has always said that it is the ones left behind who most need our prayers, I still wondered why Amma was not saying more about the deceased mother. The next time I saw the two orphaned boys, I got my answer.

It was during one of Amma's foreign tours. Amma held both the boys in her arms for a long time, kissing their foreheads, running her hands through their hair, and stroking their backs. The older boy had a question for Amma. "Where has our mother gone?"

"Your mother is with me," Amma told him. "She has merged in me forever."

I was translating for Amma at the time, and even as I faithfully translated her exact words, I remembered the scriptural quote: "Liberation comes only through *jnana*."[12] I thought to myself that this woman didn't seem to be a *jnani* (one who has attained jnana). At the same time, I immediately recalled the story, previously recounted in *Ultimate Success*, of Amma bestowing liberation on one of the family's goats when she was just a young girl. I also remembered that the 20th century mahatma Sri Ramana Maharshi gave *mukti* (liberation) to both his mother and to a cow that lived in his ashram, neither of whom had attained jnana before dying. For ordinary people, of course, the scriptural statements hold true: we cannot attain liberation without realizing our True Self before the moment of our death. But mahatmas

---

[12] Literally, "knowledge." Here, jnana refers to the knowledge of one's true nature as Brahman, the Supreme Consciousness.

are not bound by the scriptures—through the grace of a mahatma like Amma, anything is possible. Once, a man from Tamil Nadu came to see Amma with a few of his friends. During his darshan, he asked Amma, "Can you give me liberation? If so, please give me a mantra."

Amma said, "Yes, but not now... you have some more karma to exhaust in this lifetime; come later." After a few weeks the same man returned and again asked Amma for a mantra. Amma said she would give him one, but he didn't know that generally Amma gives mantras only at the end of the day's darshan, and he left without waiting. The third time he came to see Amma, he finally got the mantra.

As he was very busy as a manager of a company, he did not find much time to chant the mantra during the day. But rather than miss his chance to perform the sadhana Amma had prescribed for him, he would sit every night after midnight and chant the mantra and meditate into the early morning hours.

After that he became very interested in organizing a program for Amma in his home town in Tamil Nadu. As a prelude to that, one of Amma's brahmacharis went to give satsang there and to generate more awareness about Amma. As the devotee from Tamil Nadu was about to introduce the brahmachari to the audience, he chanted "Om Amriteswaryai Namah, Adi Parasakti, Amma, Akhilandeswaryai, Amriteswari..." (I bow down to the Immortal Goddess, Primordial Supreme Energy, Mother, Goddess of all of creation) into the microphone. As he chanted, he began to sway back and forth and finally fell backwards away from the podium. It appeared that he had become overwhelmed with devotion, and a couple of volunteers standing nearby leapt forward to attend to him. When they reached his side, they saw that he had stopped breathing. They rushed him to a nearby hospital, where he was pronounced dead on arrival. He had died chanting Amma's name.

The brahmachari who had gone for the program immediately called me and asked me to inform Amma. In those days, it was customary for the brahmacharis to chant the *Lalita Sahasranama* (1,000 Names of the Divine Mother) as a prayer for the devotee's departed soul. So when I informed Amma about the death of the devotee in Tamil Nadu and asked her if we should chant the *Lalita Sahasranama* that evening, she said, "Your prayers are not necessary—he has already reached his destination." I understood that he had merged with the Infinite.

In both cases, I knew that I had no business questioning Amma's statements about the fate of the soul since I was totally ignorant on such matters whereas Amma has clearly demonstrated that she has perfect firsthand knowledge of life after death.

Approximately twenty-five years ago, Swami Purnamritananda Puri (then Br. Sreekumar) found Amma sitting on the verandah of the old temple,[13] rapidly jotting something down in a notebook. As he approached, Amma turned away, hiding what she had been writing, and said in a stern voice, "Son, don't come near me now!"

Swami Purnamritananda meekly obeyed, but his curiosity was strongly aroused. Amma continued writing with rapt attention for more than two hours, filling two eighty-page notebooks with her script. Finally, seeing that Amma seemed to have finished, he approached her and asked, "Amma, what were you writing

---

[13] The ashram's original temple which was not much bigger than a walk-in closet and had been converted from Amma's family's cowshed. Looking back, it is amazing to consider that Amma, who now often gives programs in amphitheaters and stadiums, could ever have given darshan in such a small space.

about?" Without answering, Amma suddenly got up and left, taking the books with her.

A few months passed. One afternoon, while Swami Purnamritananda was cleaning Amma's hut, a wooden box under her bed caught his attention. He opened the box and in it were the same two notebooks that Amma had been writing in several months before. Opening one of the books and beginning to read, he was wonderstruck—in clear and beautiful prose, Amma had unraveled the secrets of the universe as if the answers were in plain view for all to see. Suddenly, from a distance, he heard Amma coming. He quickly closed the books, replaced them in the box, and pushed it back under her bed.

Swami Purnamritananda never forgot about the contents of those notebooks, and some years later when a devotee wanted to publish a collection of Amma's teachings, he went into Amma's hut, pulled the box out from under her bed, and retrieved the notebooks. Suddenly, as if out of nowhere, Amma came in, snatched the books from his hands and ran out of the hut and over to the backwaters. As he watched in disbelief, Amma tore up the notebooks, ripping out the pages, tearing them into little pieces, and flinging them into the backwaters.

However, when had Amma torn the books away from him, a few pages had remained in his hand. In those few pages Amma had depicted the journey the soul takes after death before taking rebirth in another physical form.

Since then Amma has verbally described the same process on several occasions. Amma says that when the body perishes, our soul remains intact, just as electricity lives on even after the light bulb breaks. There is a subtle aura surrounding our body; just as a tape recorder records everything we say, our aura records all our thoughts, words and actions while we are alive. After death, that aura enters the atmosphere in the shape of a balloon along with the *jiva* (individual soul). It then rises in the atmosphere like the smoke of a cigarette.

These souls are then reborn according to their karma. Coming down to earth in the form of rain or snow, they enter the earth and become one with plants. These plants, in turn, give fruit, vegetables and grains. When these foods are eaten by men, the soul then integrates into their blood. The blood becomes semen, and thus the soul finally enters the ova to take another physical body.

On the other hand, those souls who have realized the Self merge into the Infinite at the time of death like a drop of water merging into the ocean, or like a balloon bursting—the air inside becomes one with the totality. There is no rebirth for such a soul.

Just as we cannot see a transparent crystal when it is immersed in water, we are unable to see the soul. We cannot say that this means it does not exist. We have many bacteria inside our eyelids, but we are not able to see them either. Just like physics, chemistry or geology, spirituality is a science, developed by observation and verifiable by experience. Because the object of study is more subtle, the instruments required for observation are also more subtle. In fact, all spiritual practices are just a means of cleaning or purifying our inner instruments. Just as a dirty mirror does not provide a clear reflection, when our inner instruments are clouded over by thoughts and desires, we are unable to perceive the subtle reality. When we have attained *antahkarana-shuddhi* (purity of the inner instruments), the Truth is revealed in all its divine glory.

Amma's description of life after death is perfectly consistent with the teachings of the Upanishads, though she has never studied the scriptures. It is said that the Vedas, of which the Upanishads are a part, are the breath of God. The mantras comprising them were not thought up by anyone but perceived by the *rishis* (seers);

they have always existed in a subtle form in the atmosphere. Amma did not need to read the scriptures because her vision is subtle enough to perceive these truths—for Amma, the universe is an open book, and her every conversation is an Upanishad.

We may wonder why Amma would have torn up the notebooks. Only Amma knows for certain, but in contemplating her motive I was reminded of a story about Lord Shiva and his second son, Skanda (Murugan), who by divine power had memorized all the scriptures of Sanatana Dharma—a canon far too vast to assimilate in the lifetime of a human being. One day Lord Shiva approached his son and said, "As you have comprehensive knowledge of the scriptures and all the branches of Vedic science, you are also perfectly versed in the science of *jyotish* (Vedic astrology). Please, tell me what it says about my future."

Skanda obediently prepared an astrological chart for his father. Examining it for a moment, he looked up and said, "You will have two wives, no possessions to speak of, and you will spend your entire life as a homeless beggar with no place to call your own."

Hearing Skanda's prediction, Lord Shiva said, "It is true that you can accurately predict the future, but you don't know the correct way to share that information with others. Even when describing the life of your own father, you make it sound so shameful. What then will you say to ordinary human beings? Instead of presenting your predictions in a positive light, you speak indiscriminately and wound others with your words. Henceforth, even if you and all those who study the science of jyotish have all the correct information at your fingertips—time and place of birth, and the positions of the stars at that time—you will not be able to predict anything with complete accuracy."

Lord Shiva revoked from humanity the ability to predict the future with complete accuracy. In the same way, I feel that Amma, by tearing the pages of her writings, chose to withhold from us the complete picture of the way the world works. Maybe we are not ready to face it. Or maybe, as Amma once said, it would be like the prince who agrees to play blind man's bluff. Stumbling around with the blindfold over his eyes, he searches for his hidden playmates. He can easily remove the blindfold or call his friends out of hiding if wants to, as he is the prince and everyone is obliged to go along with his wishes. But then, it would take all the fun out of his game. ❖

CHAPTER 10

Restructuring Our Spiritual DNA

Speak or act with an impure mind
And trouble will follow you
As the wheel follows the ox that draws the cart.

Speak or act with a pure mind
And happiness will follow you
As your shadow, unshakable.

—Dhammapada

We all know that our present physical condition is a product of our DNA, which in turn comes from our ancestors and—short of being damaged by certain environmental agents—cannot be changed. But just imagine if it were possible over a period of time to, little by little, restructure our own DNA at will. Obviously, our physical condition would change. This is, of course, not possible for our physical DNA, but it is possible for our spiritual DNA, which is another way of referring to our accumulated karma from this and previous lifetimes.

The seed of a Giant Sequoia may be only a few grams in weight, but it carries the potential for a 2,500-ton tree. The seed is a product of the sum total of the tree—its essence—literally in a nutshell. Even if we plant it after 1,000 years, its DNA makeup determines that we will get only a Giant Sequoia; it will not grow into a banana tree.

It is the same with our karma, our spiritual DNA. Our subtle body, too, is summarized in a seed form at the time of death. When circumstances ripen, our spiritual DNA bears fruit, just like the DNA in a seed matures into a tree over time.

As human beings, we are the architects of our destiny. This is true not only individually but on a collective level as well. In a question-and-answer session during one of Amma's foreign tours, a young man asked Amma, "All around the world we see the indigenous cultures and native traditions being wiped off the face of the earth. Why would God allow this to happen?" In her answer, Amma said that God did not wipe out these cultures, human beings did. Each of us bears partial responsibility for the society in which we live. God has given us various talents and the energy to perform actions; what we do with these gifts is up to us. We can use fire to cook food or to burn down a house. If we use the pwer of fire for harmful purposes, we cannot blame the fire.

Once there was an elderly carpenter who had spent his entire career building houses but had never made enough money to purchase one of his own. Still, he wanted to spend more time with his grandchildren, and so he decided to retire.

When he told his employer of his plans to leave the house-building business, the contractor asked the old carpenter if he could build just one more house as a personal favor. The carpenter said yes, but in time it was easy to see that his heart was not in his work. He resorted to shoddy workmanship and used inferior materials. It was an unfortunate way to end his career.

Finally the carpenter finished his work, and the contractor came to inspect the house. He looked surprised to see that the carpenter had done such an uncharacteristically poor job, but he didn't comment on it. Instead, he sighed regretfully and handed the front-door key to the carpenter. "This is your house," the contractor said, "my gift to you." Realizing his mistake, the carpenter was heartbroken. His head hanging in shame, he took the keys to his new home.

If he had known he was building his own home, the carpenter would have done his work with much more sincerity and care. Now it was too late—he had to live in the house he had built.

Similarly, our life today is the result of our past thoughts, words and actions. Our life tomorrow will be the result of the choices we make today. This applies not only to this life but to our past and future lifetimes as well. Every action, whether good or bad, has an effect. A good action has a positive result (for instance, if I help somebody, someone will help me one day) and a bad action brings a negative result, either immediately or in the long run.

Just like the law of gravity, the law of karma is strict and unwavering. But with the grace of a mahatma, faith and a little effort, we can restructure our spiritual DNA and make our destiny relatively more favorable than it might have been, avoiding a great deal of suffering.

There was a devotee of Amma who was doing *seva* (selfless service) in the kitchen during one of Amma's programs in Tamil Nadu. As he was pouring boiling water from one vessel to another, his hand slipped and the water splashed over his arm. His skin began to blister immediately. After receiving first aid, he went to tell Amma what had happened. Though he did not express it to Amma at the time, inwardly he was slightly troubled by the incident. He wondered, "How could such a thing happen to me while I was doing seva for Amma?"

A week later, after Amma had returned to Amritapuri and the devotee had gone back to work, I received a phone call from his wife. She was very distraught. There had been an explosion at the factory where he worked, and several people had been rushed to the hospital with severe burn injuries. She heard that her husband was among those seriously injured, and wanted Amma's blessing to ensure that he would be alright. Not long after, however, she called again to say that, in fact, her husband had not been in the factory at the time of the accident, as he had gone out on an errand. It was a coworker by the same name who had been rushed to the hospital.

A couple of days later the devotee came in person to express his gratitude to Amma for protecting him from injury; he felt it was only due to Amma's grace that he had not been in the factory at the time of the accident.

"Why should you have gotten burned now?" Amma asked him casually. "Don't you remember what happened last week?"

Hearing Amma's words the devotee was astonished, suddenly realizing that the minor injuries he had sustained the week before while doing seva at Amma's program had been a blessing in disguise—in this way Amma had helped him to exhaust the karma that otherwise would have borne fruit in the factory fire.

When my *purvashrama*[14] sister was very young, she was afflicted with a debilitating case of rheumatism. My purvashrama parents went to many doctors and tried every available medicine, but nothing cured the disease. As almost any parents in India would, they finally consulted an astrologer seeking a spiritual cure. After reading her horoscope, the astrologer suggested conducting several large-scale fire ceremonies, requiring my parents to hire ten or

---

[14] After becoming a sannyasi, one does not refer to one's biological relatives in the usual way, as "my mother," "my sister," etc. because a sannyasi is supposed to have transcended all attachments and responsibilities to his or her biological family. When a sannyasi does refer to a biological relative, he or she will preface it with the word *purvashrama* (from my previous stage of life). For the sake of easy reading, however, this word has been omitted from all but the initial references to my biological family members.

twelve priests and provide free meals to poor Brahmins. Despite the great expense, my parents followed the astrologer's instructions and within about four months, my sister's health was restored. However, ten years later the symptoms of the disease returned. By that time, we had met Amma. Even so, my parents thought they would have to do the same old rituals to save her; the only difference being that in the intervening years, the cost of hiring the priests and arranging the elaborate ceremonies had gone up.

But this time, my sister was unwilling to participate. She felt that she could be easily cured by Amma's grace alone. When she told Amma about the problem, Amma gave her a mantra and asked her to chant it every morning and evening for thirty minutes each. She did as Amma instructed and after six months, she was fine.

The scriptures say there are actually three types of karma. *Sanchita* karma is the totality of the results arising from our actions in all our previous lifetimes. The portion of our sanchita karma which we will experience in this particular lifetime is called *prarabdha* karma and it is this that is responsible for our present birth. Whether we are a man or a woman, chronically sick or healthy as a horse, eat from silver spoons or out of a dumpster, and innumerable other factors about our life are determined by our prarabdha karma. This prarabdha karma is the spiritual DNA we bring with us into this life.

As an illustration of prarabdha karma, Amma gives the example of the case of twins, born from the same womb. Sometimes one twin is born blind, while the other is perfectly healthy. This is not something that God does deliberately. It is the result of their actions performed in past births. Similarly, it is due to the prarabdha of the mother and father that such a child is born to them.

While living this life, we not only fulfill our prarabdha karma, we also undertake many new actions. The results of the actions we perform in our present existence are added to our credit and are called *agami* karma. Much of this agami karma will bear fruit in this life. The rest will be added to our sanchita karma after death. When the prarabdha karma is exhausted, the body dies.

After the death of our body, another portion of sanchita karma becomes the prarabdha karma of our next birth. In that new incarnation, we will create more agami karma and we will again have to be reborn to discharge it. This is *samsara*, or the cycle of birth and death. All beings who remain ignorant of their True Self are caught up in this repetitive cycle.

Amma says that just as there are physical laws like the laws of gravity and floatation, there are subtle spiritual laws as well. The law of karma is one such law. If we are aware of the law of gravity, we will be careful not to drop anything. If we are similarly aware of the law of karma, we will be careful in our every thought, word, and action. In this way we can restructure our spiritual DNA and create a future for ourselves that is more and more conducive to spiritual progress.

When one attains Self-realization, the agami karma and sanchita karma are instantaneously wiped out because the liberated soul realizes that he is the Atman, the eternal witness. Even if we are sitting in the driver's seat, we cannot drive if there is no fuel in the car. At the same time, if we get in a wreck, we can't blame the fuel. Similarly, it is only in the presence of the Atman that the body, mind and intellect can function, but the Atman itself is not doing anything. The Atman never performs any actions and therefore never accrues any karma.

Because the Self-realized person is identified with the Atman, whatever actions he performs after attaining realization will not create any new karma for him. After realizing the Self, only the prarabdha karma that is attached to the present existence remains. When that is exhausted, the body falls off. Such liberated souls are released from the cycle of birth and death.[15]

Even if we are not able to attain liberation in this birth, we can at least avoid adding to our burden of sanchita karma by not creating additional agami karma. For this we must learn to perform actions without *kartrutva bodham*, or the feeling, "I am the doer." The easiest way to transcend this feeling is to consider ourselves as an instrument of God. Amma says we should see ourselves as a pen in the hands of a divine writer, or a brush in the hands of a divine painter.

As long as we act with the feeling, "I am the doer," or the desire to enjoy the fruits of our efforts, we will continue to accumulate karma. This chain of karma is what keeps us trapped in the cycle of birth and death. If we make our actions an offering to God, however, we will not be bound by these actions, nor by their results—everything belongs to Him. Of course we cannot harm others or perform other negative actions and justify them saying, "I am not the doer—God does everything." The scriptures of all religions always exhort us to be loving and compassionate toward others, and to behave in a righteous and virtuous way. If we act against God's instructions, we cannot blame God for what we have done.

Amma says that when we succeed, we take all the credit, quick to point out that it was "I" who did it, "I" who made it happen.

---

[15] However, by their own will they may take another birth for the purpose of blessing the world, helping suffering humanity, and guiding spiritual seekers toward liberation. Amma always says that she is ready to take any number of births for the sake of her children.

When our efforts meet with failure, even if it is due to our own mistake, we point our finger in the opposite direction.

An elderly man was driving down the freeway when his mobile phone rang. It was his wife. She said in a panicked tone, "Henry, I just heard on the news that there's a car going the wrong way on the freeway. Please be careful, honey!"

"I don't know where they get their facts," Henry complained. "It's not just one car—it's hundreds of them!"

We might think, "Why should I put everything in God's hands? It is my talents and my abilities that have allowed me to be successful." But it is exactly this attitude that binds us to our actions and their ensuing results.

At Amma's ashram, many people work very hard without expecting anything in return. We work for hours every day without getting any salary and we are happy to be able to offer all these efforts to Amma and to the world. These efforts are indeed laudable. However, though we have certainly performed our tasks with dedication and love, some of us may still have the feeling, "It is I who did it; it is I who have done so much for Amma." Instead, we should try to cultivate the attitude, "Whatever I am doing, it is God's strength which allows me to do it." In this way we can reap the full benefit of selfless action—rather than reaching the heavens, we can eliminate the ego and thus go beyond merit and demerit, heaven and hell, and attain the purity of mind that is a fundamental prerequisite of our final liberation.

In ancient times there lived a benign yet powerful emperor by the name of Mahabali who had conquered all the worlds and the heavens too. His reign was a golden age, wherein his subjects were happy and content. Their lives were free of worry. In talking about her childhood days and the celebration of Onam, a festival dedicated to the memory of Mahabali's reign, Amma recalls that the children from about fifty or sixty households in each village would assemble in the courtyard where they would put up a big swing and sing songs of Mahabali, like:

maveli nāṭuvānīṭuṁ kālaṁ
mānuṣarellārūm onnupōle

During the time when Mahabali was ruling the country all of humankind lived as one.

Though Mahabali had done so many good works and his empire was peaceful, he was a man full of pride in his great achievements. In order to correct his attitude so that it did not hinder his spiritual evolution, Lord Vishnu decided to intervene. The Lord incarnated in the form of a young brahmachari named Vamana and visited the emperor. When a guest arrives, Hindu tradition requires that he is honored as God Himself and that he leaves satisfied. Thus, upon his arrival at the palace, Mahabali inquired of the small boy what it was he might be wanting. Vamana answered: "I wish only for as much land as may be covered by three of my steps, so that I can practice my austerities there."

Full of conceit, the emperor thought, "What are three steps of land for me, the ruler of so many worlds?" With a condescending look, he declared, "Is that all you want? I could give you three countries!"

"No," replied Vamana. "Three steps of land are all I require."

With a disdainful shake of his head, Mahabali pronounced, "Well, then… I give you the three steps of land—take them!" Precisely at that moment, the boy Vamana began to grow in size. He grew and grew until his head, then his shoulders and finally his entire body down to his ankles had passed above the clouds. With his first step, he strode over the whole Earth, and with the second, he covered the worlds of heaven above. Then his voice boomed out from on high, "Your Majesty, where can I take my third step?"

Realizing that it could only be a divine incarnation standing before him, the great emperor bowed low and said, "O Lord, deign to place your foot upon my head."

Although summarized only briefly here, this story is full of spiritual symbolism.

With his first step, Lord Vishnu took from Mahabali the whole world, thereby destroying the emperor's *mamakara*, or sense of "mine," which manifested as his attachment to his empire.

Mahabali had accomplished wonderful things. He was recognized as one of the most charitable and righteous rulers in the history of the world; therefore, he had gained a lot of merit. But, considering himself as the performer of his actions and the source of all his power, Mahabali harbored an immense pride. Therefore, he was binding himself to his actions and their consequences. As long as he maintained the attitude that he was the doer, he would have to continue taking birth again and again to exhaust the karma he was creating for himself. Even though it might be good karma, allowing Mahabali to reincarnate in the upper worlds, it would not free him from the cycle of birth and death. By taking his second step in the heavenly realms, however, Vishnu annulled all of Mahabali's accumulated merit. The emperor would no longer have to exhaust his good karma by taking birth in the upper worlds, full of limited pleasures; he would be able to merge directly in the infinite.

With the third step, when he placed his foot on the king's head, Lord Vishnu destroyed his sense of ego, or *ahamkara*, and Mahabali attained liberation. ❖

CHAPTER 11

On Giving and Self-Sacrifice

How far that little candle throws his beams! So shines a good deed in a weary world.

—William Shakespeare

Recently I heard the story of a little girl who was suffering from a rare and serious disease. Her only chance of recovery was to receive a blood transfusion from her five-year-old brother, who had barely managed to survive the same disease the year before. In the process, his body had developed the antibodies needed to combat the illness.

The doctor explained the situation to her brother, and asked the little boy if he would be willing to give his blood to his sister. The boy hesitated for only a moment before taking a deep breath and saying, "Yes. If it will save my sister, I'll do it."

As the transfusion progressed, he lay in bed next to his sister and smiled, as did the rest of the family, seeing the color returning to the girl's cheeks. But slowly the boy's face grew pale and his smile faded. He looked up at the doctor and asked with a trembling voice, "Will I start to die right away?"

The little boy had misunderstood the doctor; he thought he was going to have to give his sister *all* of his blood in order to save her.

The innocent attitude with which this little boy was ready to give up his life for his sister is very exceptional in today's world.

While many people do good works, it is rare to find someone doing charity with a pure heart.

When Amma was young, she once saw her brother giving clothes to a poor man, but instead of handing them to him, he threw the clothes to him. When her family served the food to the very poor (back then, considered untouchable), they would just put it down and go away. Her family knew that in order to receive God's grace one should serve the poor, but they did not understand the underlying principle. When they saw Amma bathing the poor, feeding them and comforting them with her own hands, initially they were shocked and appalled. Slowly, Amma led them to understand the principle behind these acts of service: service to the poor is service to God, because God is in the poor—God is everywhere. Now, her family members have all become her devotees, and many of them are doing selfless service in the ashram's charitable institutions.

The *Taittiriya Upanishad* describes the correct attitude that must accompany a charitable action for it to be considered one attracting the most merit and grace.

> *śraddhayā deyam, aśraddhayā-deyam*
> *śriyā deyam hriyā deyam*
> *bhiyā deyam, saṁvidā deyam*
>
> *Gifts should be given with faith and never without faith.*
> *Gifts should be given in plenty, with modesty and with fear.*
> *Gifts should be given with understanding.*

(1.11.5)

Here, to give with faith means that we should have faith in the cause we are supporting. We should not give out of a sense of obligation, but because we believe in our heart it is the right thing to do. To give with modesty means that we should never be arrogant about our ability to give. We should always remember that there are others who are able to give more than we, and that in truth everything belongs to God—the opportunity to serve others is a precious gift from God. Even with all that Amma has done for the world, she says humbly, "God alone does all this. I am not doing anything. If God gives me the strength, I can act."

What does it mean to give with fear? We must always be on our guard against the ego. If we do a good deed, we tend to feel proud of ourselves, thereby reinforcing our ego. In this way the very acts that are intended to weaken and finally eliminate the ego only serve to make it bigger and stronger.

Samvida deyam can be interpreted in a number of ways. It can mean that using our discrimination, we ensure that the gift is going to a deserving person who will make proper use of it. It can also mean to give with jnana, or the knowledge that all beings in the universe are different forms of the same divine essence, and that when we help someone, we are serving God.

Our usual idea about charity and sacrifice is actually quite distorted. We make our so-called sacrifices begrudgingly, thinking, "Oh, no, I have to give up something *again*." But the origin of the word "sacrifice," even in English, is something else altogether. It comes from the Latin *sacrificium*, which means, "to make sacred." This is precisely the concept behind sacrifice: whatever it may be, by offering it to God, it becomes sacred, and the results come back to us as *prasad*.[16]

In the *Bhagavad Gita* (3.15), Sri Krishna tells Arjuna that sacrifice is an integral part of creation. This is because we are always sacrificing one thing for another—it is just a question of

---

[16] Any item that has been blessed by or offeredto the satguru or God is called prasad.

whether we are sacrificing the lower for the higher or the higher for the lower. Every day, we act as the chief priest overseeing the temple of our life, making the offerings of our every thought, word, and action, on the altar of some goal or aspiration, be it high or low. Amma says that, unfortunately, we are too often sacrificing the higher for the lower. In this way, our humane qualities—and along with them, our opportunity to attain inner peace—are being sacrificed for the sake of temporary gains and pleasures.

Once a man approached a sannyasi with folded palms. "O Swamiji," he began. "I pay my respects to you, for you have sacrificed so much."

The sannyasi replied, "In fact I should bow down to you, for your sacrifice is greater than mine."

The man was taken aback. "How can you say that, Swamiji? I live in a comfortable house with my family and whatever I desire I can easily acquire."

"It's true that I have renounced the pleasures of this world, but I did so for the sake of obtaining eternal peace, whereas you have willingly sacrificed your peace of mind in exchange for all the problems and woes of worldly life. Whose sacrifice, then, is the greater one?"

If we closely observe and emulate Amma, we can learn how to make our sacrifice one of the lower for the higher, rather than vice versa.

A few years ago, during one of Amma's programs in Chennai, a leper came for Amma's darshan. After she had embraced him, someone nearby asked Amma how she could take such a risk. "I could never even think of doing such a thing," the person confessed to Amma.

Amma explained, "Whenever I am faced with such situations, I ask myself: 'Am I living for myself, or for the world? If I am living for myself, I shouldn't do it. But I am living for the world, so I must.'" (Of course, such doubts never occur to Amma, but she puts it this way in order to set an example we can relate to.) This shows the strength of Amma's unshakeable conviction in putting the needs of others before her own.

I remember another conversation that took place a few years ago at Amma's ashram in India. Swami Jnanamritananda Puri was first put in charge of the printing press, then also the monthly spiritual magazine. On top of that Amma asked him to look after the schools for some time, then some of the newer charitable projects, and his workload went on increasing, even up to the present day.

Though he did not mind the workload, attending to the day-to-day affairs of the various projects meant that his attention was directed outward for much of the day, whereas he felt a strong inclination to withdraw his attention from the world completely. When he had a chance to talk with Amma, he mentioned this to her. "I just want to drop everything for a while, go to an isolated place and immerse myself in meditation."

When Amma heard his words, her face lit up and she replied, "You know, I feel like that sometimes, too! But I offered this life for the sake of the whole world long ago, so my individual concerns no longer matter. There is no longer any 'I' to drop the work, or a 'myself' to sit in an isolated place. Everything is for the sake of the world."

Amma compassionately identified with the swami's feelings, but also showed him how to go beyond them. Hearing Amma's words, he felt a renewed enthusiasm to carry out his duties with an attitude of self-surrender.

Amma is greatly appreciative of the sacrifices made by her children for the sake of the world. "We should write a book about each and every person," she once commented. "Someone should also make a documentary about Amma's disciples and devotees in India and abroad who are tirelessly working for the sake of others—such a documentary would inspire the future generations."

Amma says, "We should be like candles that give light to the world even as they melt down and burn away." When the wax candle burns, it does not melt into nothingness but becomes fuel for the flame. Without the liquid wax, the flame would not exist; the wax, in achieving a subtler state, becomes part of the flame. Just as the function of the candle is to merge into the flame, the culmination of the mind's function is to merge into God.

Amma says, "Real spiritual seekers wish to serve others through sacrifice. Their goal is to have a mind that gives joy to others while forgetting its own struggles. They pray for that. Amma is waiting for such individuals. Liberation comes in search of them and will wait on them like a servant maid."

If we want to know the real meaning of sacrifice, we need look no further than Amma. Amma is the North Star of sacrifice and service, showing us both the direction and the goal. In terms of her dedication, Amma has set a record that can never be broken—Amma works twenty-four hours a day. Unless they invent a longer day, no one can possibly do more than Amma is doing to uplift the world. And while we can never live up to Amma's example, we can always keep it before us as a guide.

One night one of the brahmacharis passed by Amma's room at about 3:30 in the morning and noticed a tiny glow of light emanating from one corner of the room. The next day, when he inquired about it, Amma's attendant confessed that Amma had been up all night reading letters from her devotees around the world. Because the swamis had been expressing their concern about Amma staying up too late and not getting any rest, Amma had been using a flashlight to read the letters so that we wouldn't see her lights on and notice she was still awake.

Amma always gives priority to the devotees' happiness, even at the expense of her own health and comfort.

Once, during a tour in India, Amma was scheduled to visit a particular devotee's house after a darshan program. Because the crowd for darshan was bigger than expected, Amma was late by several hours, and the hosts had to wait for a long time. They had prepared a special meal for Amma with great love, and were eagerly waiting for her to taste the dishes. Finally Amma arrived, and after performing a short *puja* (ritual worship), she proceeded to the dining room to distribute prasad. The hosts had kept aside a special container with Amma's food inside, but when one of the brahmacharis opened it for Amma, he could immediately tell that the food had gone bad. He whispered to Amma, "Amma, this food is spoiled—don't eat it!"

Amma gestured for him to keep quiet and began eating the dish with great relish, all the while knowing that it was spoiled and that she could get sick as a result. After a few spoonfuls, she closed the lid and said, "Amma likes this very much, so she will take it with her and have the rest later." Then she distributed the food, which had been cooked for the swamis and had not spoiled, as prasad to the devotees. Later, in the car, she remarked, "It's true that the food was spoiled, but if the hosts had found out, they would have been terribly sad. Amma took it with her so that others wouldn't get sick from eating it."

In May of 2006, Amma was presented with the 2006 James Parks Morton Interfaith Award at the Interfaith Center in New York City. As part of the award ceremony, Amma delivered an address on inter-religious understanding and collaboration.

Before Amma left the ashram in India to attend the conference, she held a question-and-answer session with the ashram residents. Amma regularly gives such opportunities for them to clear their doubts and receive her guidance. On that particular day, the ashram residents had only one question. They wanted Amma to talk about the award she was going to receive in New York. Amma's response tells us a lot about her perspective on life. She said, "Amma has not given any thought to the award; Amma is not going to New York to receive an award but because the Interfaith Center has requested her to give an address." Amma continued, "The greatest award that Amma can receive is the happiness of her children; Amma doesn't want any other award."

For most of the ashram residents, all the focus had been on what Amma was going to receive in New York, whereas Amma was totally focused on what she was going to give. This desire to give is the focus of Amma's entire life. Amma says, "Most people are concerned only with what they can get from the world, but it is what we are able to give to others that determines the quality of our life." ❀

CHAPTER 12

From Anger to Compassion

For every minute you remain angry, you give up sixty seconds of peace of mind.

—Ralph Waldo Emerson

As she does every year, in February and March of 2006, Amma completed a tour of India from the South to the northernmost states, giving programs in seventeen cities. It goes without saying that anyone else in Amma's position would have flown between tour stops and used the extra time to catch up on rest. The crowds have gotten much bigger over the years, sometimes drawing hundreds of thousands of people and leaving only very limited traveling time. Even so, Amma insisted on driving this year as in previous years, only to give some of her time to the ashram residents and devotees who were accompanying her on the tour. Some of these grueling drives took twenty-four hours or more; on some rides the roads were so rough that it seemed we would have made better time on foot.

At the outset of another drive that promised to be particularly long and arduous, Amma announced that she wanted to visit a devotee's house—more than an hour out of the way. Knowing that Amma had not rested, much less slept in more than twenty-four hours, a number of the brahmacharis tried to talk Amma out of making the stop. When they found that Amma could not be swayed, some of them became quite upset toward the man who had invited Amma to his house, feeling that he was very selfish and simply did not care whether or not Amma got any rest.

When Amma reached the house, she sat in front of the family's altar and performed a puja, after which she sang a bhajan. The longer it took, the angrier the brahmacharis felt toward the host. When Amma finished the worship, she went into one of the bedrooms in order to speak with the man and his wife privately. A few of the brahmacharis followed her. Once inside, their anger evaporated instantly.

A boy of about ten years old lay on the bed, his body terribly deformed. His head was misshapen and gigantic in proportion to his body. His limbs were no more than skin stretched over bone, totally devoid of fat or muscle. His hands curled inward to the point of being useless. His wandering eyes would open no more than a slit, but with no control over his head, neck, or the direction of his gaze, it wouldn't have done him much good anyway. Everything about his existence looked agonizing. His mother knelt by his side and cradled him under her arms. At this, the boy began to scream. There was no way he could lift his head on his own, and even with help it was obviously an excruciating experience. It was clear that the boy's parents could not have brought him out of the house, even to receive Amma's darshan.

There wasn't a dry eye in the room—the mother, the father, Amma, even the brahmacharis who had been so angry a few moments before could not hold back their tears as Amma embraced the child, caressing his chest and kissing his forehead. The agony of the child's existence was reflected in the deep concern and empathy in Amma's eyes.

"I have been praying for the past three years that Amma would come and bless my child," the boy's father confessed, his cheeks streaked with tears.

"We feel love and compassion toward people only when we stand in their shoes and try to understand their problems and situation," Amma often says. "Anger converts into compassion when we properly understand a situation." A satguru not only teaches his disciples through words but creates situations so that his disciples can come to understand the truth of the master's words in their hearts. Such experiences are never forgotten.

Amma says that when we see someone commit a mistake, instead of passing judgment or preparing to punish them, we should try to look at the situation from their perspective and try to understand what motivated them to act in the way they did. Amma tells the following story.

Once, a woman went to a park with her two children. She allowed the kids to play while she sat on a bench alone. The children were delighted and began to run around and make a lot of noise. A man who was also visiting the park was very annoyed at their behavior. "Look, lady," he complained to the children's mother. "Your children are disturbing those of us who would like to enjoy some peace and quiet. Why can't you make your kids behave themselves?"

The woman did not reply to his tirade, but continued to sit silently with her face buried in her hands. The man was a little surprised, and asked her if she was alright. Finally she looked up and he saw that her cheeks were streaked with tears. "A few minutes ago, my husband—my children's father—died in an accident while traveling abroad. I have no idea how to break the news to my children, or how I could possibly console them. I just came here to collect myself and try to figure out how to explain what has happened." Hearing this, the man felt ashamed of his rash words and apologized to her for his lack of understanding. Overwhelmed with sympathy, he made every effort to be kind and helpful to the widow and her children. To give her some more time to gather her strength, he even took the children out for ice cream before driving them home.

Anger is not an action, but a reaction. It is not so difficult to avoid performing an action, but to overcome reactions is much more difficult and requires a high level of awareness. For example, suppose you are standing across the room, and I ask you to come closer. You may come, you may not come or you may even walk away. Thus regarding any action, we have three choices—to take the action, to refrain from the action, or to do the opposite. But this is not the case with reactions. Without a high level of awareness, we have no choice at all in the matter of how we react to a particular situation. For example, if I politely ask you to get angry with me, it will not be possible for you. On the other hand, if I shout at you or blame you for something you didn't do, in most cases it will be impossible for you *not* to get angry with me. This is because anger is not an action that we can perform at will, but a reaction. It happens almost automatically. There is a small window of opportunity to avoid it—spiritual practices help us to open this window wide. Through spiritual practices we gain greater power of concentration; this in turn increases our awareness of what is going on both within us and in the world around us. A highly trained martial artist is able to easily defeat his enemies because, from his perspective of heightened awareness, they all seem to be moving in slow motion. Likewise after performing regular meditation and other spiritual practices for an extended period of time, we find that we become aware of the first sign of negativity arising in us, and we can use our discrimination to avoid speaking from or acting on these negative feelings.

Some years ago, I was standing near Amma when an elderly woman came for her darshan. As it was a very big crowd that day,

Amma was giving darshan very fast. After the elderly woman's darshan was over, she was having difficulty getting up and making space for the next person to come for darshan. Because I didn't want Amma to have to wait, I tried to help the woman stand and move away from Amma, but in my impatience I was a bit rough with her. Amma stopped what she was doing and looked up at me with a question. "Would you have done the same thing if it was your own grandmother?" I had no answer but to hang my head in shame.

Ultimately, Amma says that when we feel angry toward another person, we should remember that the Self in us is the same as the Self in the other person. When this is the case, who is there to get angry at whom?

The *Isavasya Upanishad* says,

yastu sarvāni bhutānyātmanyeva anupaśyati
sarvabhuteṣu cātmanam tato na vijugupsate

He who sees all beings in his own Self
and his own Self in all beings,
by virtue of that realization, feels no hatred.

yasmin sarvani bhutanyātmaivābhudvijānataḥ
tatra ko mohaḥ kaḥ śoka ekatvamanupaśyataḥ

He who has known that all beings
have become one with his own Self,
and he who has seen the oneness of existence,
what sorrow and what delusion can overwhelm him?

(6,7)

On one of Amma's Indian tours, she visited a particular city for the first time. And while it wasn't the first time that more than 100,000 people have come to one of Amma's programs, it was the first time that all of them tried to come for darshan at the exact same time.

For the entire duration of darshan, the brahmacharis, brahmacharinis and devotees traveling with Amma had to police the boundaries of the stage to prevent a stampede. In fact, the situation was such that Amma's satsang and bhajans were delayed for almost half an hour simply because no one would leave the stage. At one point during darshan, Amma herself stood up and spoke over the sound-system, telling everyone not to worry, that she would give darshan to everyone, but that they had to be patient and not push. Later, Amma commented that in thirty-five years of giving darshan, nothing like this had ever happened before.

On the way to Amma's next program, a discussion about the previous day's darshan ensued. One woman explained how at one point she had held onto a man's shirt-collar to prevent him from walking on to the stage, only to suddenly find herself holding the shirt—minus the man!

The situation there was so wild that many people told Amma she should never return to that place. One brahmachari told Amma that he had a suggestion for the spiritual evolvement of the people of that city: "Amma, I feel the ideal path for them is that of devotion," he said. "Just like the *gopis* (cowherd girls) of Vrindavan, they should spend their whole lives yearning for the Lord to return... but she never does."

Amma laughed, but indicated that she felt otherwise: "They had devotion but no knowledge," Amma explained. "Where there is darkness, they need more light. We should go there more often!"

While the devotees traveling with Amma had been highly critical of the devotees' behavior, Amma was able to put herself in their shoes and understand their attitude.

Amma always says that anger is a disability. Just as a physically disabled person is not able to move without difficulty, a short-tempered person is unable to interact freely with others—their temper will always flare up and poison their relationships. And sometimes we find that some of those who have severe physical disabilities are chronically angry. They cannot blame anyone in particular for their suffering, so they get angry with God. In some cases this anger is so all-consuming that they are unable to accomplish even what would have otherwise been possible for them with their disability. Thus they are disabled twice over—first by their physical impairment, and again by anger. There is a boy who lives at the ashram now who was born partially deaf. At the same time, he had a congenital heart disease that made it difficult for him to attend school. Throughout his education, he performed very badly, even though he was provided with the necessary tutoring and special assistance that would have enabled him to succeed. His family and tutors assumed that he was just not very bright. In fact, he was filled with resentment for having been born with disabilities, and he was just not interested in putting forth the effort to succeed. When he was eleven years old, his family met Amma and ultimately decided to move to the ashram. There Amma showed him a great deal of love and encouragement and rekindled his faith in God. Seeing how much Amma had done for him and how hard she was working to give happiness to others, he finally approached Amma and asked her if he could also do some seva at the ashram. Amma asked him to help the brahmachari in charge of the ashram's fax and photocopy office. Having been given this responsibility by Amma herself, he took it very seriously and dedicated himself wholeheartedly to learning all about the operation of the machines and the software needed for the job. Now, he knows even more about the work than the brahmachari in charge of the office, and the brahmachari refers all the most complicated jobs to this very talented young man. In the course of his work, he interacts with many of the international visitors to the ashram, and he has even picked up a working knowledge of English in addition to his mother tongue.

Amma tells the following story.

Once, there was a little girl whose legs were paralyzed. She was destined to remain in a wheelchair for her entire life. This little girl used to watch other children playing every day in the playground near her house. Because she was unable to join in their play, she always felt sad about her plight.

One day, as the girl was looking out of the window, it started raining even as the sun was shining. A beautiful rainbow appeared, and the little girl became overjoyed to see it. She even forgot her own sadness and pain. After a few moments, though, the rainbow vanished. The girl's sorrow returned and she hoped that the rainbow would appear again soon.

Every day, she would gaze into the sky expectantly, but the rainbow never appeared. Finally the girl approached her mother asking, "Mom, when will I be able to see the rainbow again?"

The mother consoled her daughter saying, "My child, when it rains and the sun shines at the same time, the rainbow will appear again." The little girl continued waiting in anticipation.

In doing so, she forgot much of her pain and suffering. Even though she still saw the children playing in the nearby playground, she stopped feeling sad about her disability. Instead, she was filled with hope and expectation that the beautiful rainbow would soon appear again.

Finally the day came when it started raining while the sun was still shining, and the rainbow appeared again. The little girl was so excited. She wanted to go as close to the rainbow as she could, and she insisted that her mother take her near the rainbow. The mother knew the rainbow would disappear very soon. Still, she did not want to disappoint her daughter. So they drove down the streets, and finally the mother told the daughter, "Let's stop here. From here, we have a beautiful view."

The little girl stared up at the rainbow in rapture. In a soft and gentle voice, she asked, "O Rainbow, how did you ever become so beautiful?"

The rainbow replied, "I used to be as sad as you. I used to feel pained at heart seeing all the scenes of celebration around me, knowing I had such a short time to live. But one day I thought to myself, 'Why should I feel unhappy? Why should I be sad? Although I only appear for a few seconds, I can use that short period of time to make others happy. I should forget my sadness and make others happy.' When that thought arose, I became more and more beautiful. Just the thought of making others happy made me so colorful."

Even as the rainbow was talking to the girl, it was slowly vanishing. When it had completely disappeared, the little girl decided: "Like the rainbow, instead of feeling sorry for myself, I, too, will try my best to make others happy."

We may be able to think of countless reasons for feeling sad, upset or depressed. Instead of brooding over our own problems, let us think about what we can offer to the world. If we have the right attitude and the grace of a true master like Amma, we can transform our negative qualities like anger, resentment and hatred into love and compassion. ❖

CHAPTER 13

The Greatest Miracle is a Change of Heart

"God creates out of nothing. Wonderful, you say. Yes, to be sure, but he does what is still more wonderful: he makes saints out of sinners."

—Søren Kierkegaard

Before we came to live with Amma, there were so many things that we would never have considered doing. Generally, in a traditional Indian household, the mother will not allow the sons to do any of the household work. We never imagined that we would carry sand bags in the middle of the night, clean toilets used by hundreds of people, or stand thigh-deep and barefoot in a septic tank. Before coming to Amma, even if someone had offered us a fortune to do these things, we would not have accepted. And yet, suddenly, we found ourselves doing it gladly. In Amma's presence, we forgot everything and were able to go beyond our prior conditioning.

Though they might initially experience difficulties, many devotees renounce their attachment to food and other comforts to live in Amma's presence. Things that would have posed great problems for them before coming to Amma now do not affect them in the least. I recall an incident from one of Amma's Indian tours which dramatically illustrates this change in outlook.

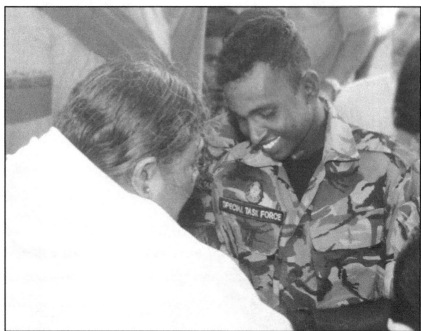

When Amma visited a tsunami relief camp in Sri Lanka, members of both the Sri Lankan Army and the LTTE (Tamil Tigers) came for Amma's darshan.

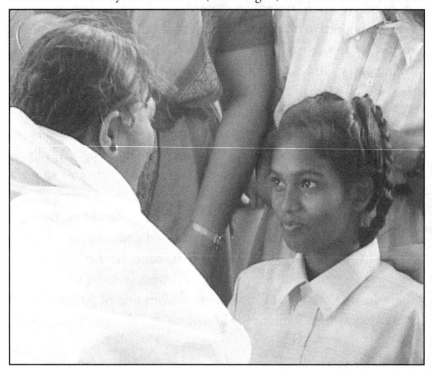

A stomach virus was circulating through the tour group. It was easily cured with a short round of antibiotics, but left untreated, it would cause terrible diarrhea. One man on the tour failed to tell the doctor of his symptoms, thinking his condition was sure to improve. However, on the next bus trip, as he made his way out of the bus for a bathroom break, he lost control of his bowels. Needless to say, it was a very embarrassing moment for him, but his bus mates were all very compassionate toward him. As a few of the men took him to a private place to get cleaned up, the rest of the passengers filed off the bus. One would expect, of course, that an argument would have ensued about who would have to clean up the mess. The bus driver? Surely he would resign his post before taking on such a loathsome task. So who would it be? Would they flip a coin, draw straws, or call a cleaning service?

In fact a debate did ensue, but, the bus being full of Amma's children, it was an altogether different sort of argument. Everyone was arguing that he should be the only one to board the bus and clean it out, and they climbed over each other in eagerness to serve one another in this way. In the end, it was a group effort, and almost everyone participated—carrying buckets of water from a nearby well, sprinkling soap, sweeping, scrubbing, mopping and finally drying off the floor of the bus. In the end, the bus was cleaner than it had been to begin with, and so were the hearts and minds of the passengers.

Of course, in most cases such a transformation does not take place overnight. Amma comments that often when a person joins the ashram as a brahmachari or brahmacharini, at first the individual expects to be assigned a seva that pleases them. Amma tells the following story to illustrate this point.

Once, a man approached a guru with folded palms. The man proclaimed that he was fed up with all that the world had to offer and wanted to spend the remainder of his life serving the guru.

"Is that so?" the guru replied. "How would you like to serve me?"

"If you permit me," the man said in a respectful tone, "I would like to serve as your advisor."

One might be highly educated or have worked in management overseeing many people, but initially Amma may ask one to work in the cowshed, shoveling manure and bathing and feeding the cows. Amma says that in fact, the seva assigned by the guru is only to help one transcend one's likes and dislikes. To that end, the guru will specifically assign one something he knows one would not have chosen on one's own.

In my first years as a brahmachari, though I was already staying in the ashram, Amma asked me to continue my job as a banker. When Amma finally did permit me to resign the position, I was happy and relieved thinking that I would now be able to do more spiritual practices like the other brahmacharis in the ashram. Around that time, someone donated a van to the ashram, and Amma chose me to be the van's driver, as I was the only ashram resident at that time who was holding a valid driver's license. I was happy to drive Amma and the brahmacharis whenever they went out to give programs. At the same time, however, Amma put me in charge of purchasing food and other supplies for the ashram. This meant that I was driving almost every day. Gone were my dreams of spending long hours immersed in spiritual practice. Of course, I was participating in most of the regular spiritual activities that were part of the ashram routine, including chanting, meditation, scriptural study and devotional singing. It was my desire to do even more than the prescribed number of hours of all these practices, but while driving, of course, it was not possible to do anything other than repeat the mantra that Amma had given me.

Several years later, a few of the other brahmacharis obtained driver's licenses. My driving days were over, and I once again rejoiced at the opportunity to become more introverted. By that time, Amma had already started her world tours, and devotees from many countries had started visiting the ashram. It was then that Amma asked me to greet and mingle with the international visitors. She told me to spend at least five hours daily talking with people and offering assistance to them. "Amma, I had planned to spend more time in meditation and other spiritual practices when I didn't have to drive anymore," I told her. "Now you are asking me to spend five hours a day talking to people—what about my *sadhana* (spiritual practice)?"

"That is your sadhana," Amma responded.

Though I was initially hesitant, I found that the devotees primarily only wanted to talk about one thing, and that was Amma. This helped me to keep my focus on Amma throughout the day. You may have heard of walking meditation, but what Amma had instructed me to do was surely a new form of sadhana—that of "talking meditation."

Like this, whatever the guru asks us to do becomes our sadhana, and simply following the guru's instructions with sincerity and dedication is just as beneficial as other spiritual practices.

Until a few years ago, I would usually perform the *arati*[17] to Amma at the beginning of the Devi Bhava darshan on her foreign tours. One day, Amma said that some people were upset about

---

[17] Arati is traditionally performed near the end of a ritual worship, and consists of waving burning camphor before the object of worship. Arati symbolizes surrender—just as the camphor used in the ritual burns away

the fact that it was always a swami doing the arati and never a swamini or brahmacharini. In consideration of their viewpoint, Amma said that from that day onwards Swamini Krishnamrita Prana should perform the arati at the beginning of every Devi Bhava.

As I had really enjoyed doing the arati to Amma, I was a little disappointed about losing the position. Of course, I accepted Amma's instructions with a positive frame of mind, remembering that, whether we like it or not, we always benefit from following the instructions of a true master.

Amma says that if we go to a doctor with an infected wound, he will have to extract the pus. We will feel some pain, but it is for our own good. Even if we cry out, a good doctor will continue to drain the wound because he knows that if left alone it will worsen and develop into a serious problem. Similarly, we are all suffering from the sickness of samsara; that is why we have come to Amma in the first place. When we come to Amma with the intention of realizing our True Self, it becomes Amma's duty to remove the negativity in us. This process is naturally painful; at times Amma will say something that hurts our ego, or ask us to do exactly the opposite of what we want to do. However, we should not resist such situations; we should accept Amma's treatment with the knowledge that it is going to make us better. We regularly undergo such situations at work, even though our boss may not be a spiritual person and is almost certainly not going to shower us with divine grace. Why then can't we happily undergo this process at the hands of Amma? The true master will never ask us to do something against dharma, and the reward will be

---

without a trace, so too does the ego dissolve completely in the process of surrendering to the guru or God.

greater than what we receive in the office. Amma's only purpose is to bring out the divinity in us.

Regarding the best way to accept the master's discipline, Amma tells a story about Sri Rama and his beloved disciple Hanuman.

Once the sage Vishwamithra ordered Sri Rama to kill a king who had inadvertently offended the sage. The king was a righteous man and Sri Rama was not happy about the instruction, but Vishwamithra was a guru for him, and he could not disobey him.

Thus he set out to fulfill Vishwamithra's request. When the threatened king heard the news, he rushed to Anjana Devi, Hanuman's mother, and asked for her protection. Even before asking what the danger was, she granted it to him, saying, "Don't worry, my lord, my son Hanuman will protect you from all danger."

However, when the king confessed that it was Lord Rama himself who wanted to kill him, Anjana Devi began to have second thoughts, for she could not bear the thought of her son doing battle with the Lord himself. But Hanuman would not allow her to go back on her word. "It's our duty to protect whoever seeks our refuge," he told his mother. "I shall not allow any harm to come to the king. We must face whoever happens to be his enemy."

Thus it was that Hanuman accosted Sri Rama in his search for the king. He fell at the feet of Rama, crying, "My Lord, please be kind to the king! Don't kill him—he is innocent. Let him go free."

But Rama was not willing to forgive the king. "I must kill him. That's the promise I made, and I cannot break it."

"I understand your devotion and loyalty to your guru," said Hanuman. "But my mother has given him a promise that she'll protect him. I'm duty-bound to keep that promise. So, if you wish to kill the king, then you must first kill me! As long as there is a breath of life left in this body, I shall not allow the king to be killed."

Sri Rama strung his bow and prepared to shower Hanuman with his arrows. However, Hanuman did not take up arms or even hold a shield. Rather, he stood with palms folded and, as always, continued chanting Rama's name. Bound to keep his word, however, the Lord began to fire volley after volley of arrows at his devotee.

Though Sri Rama had never missed his mark, not a single arrow struck Hanuman's frame, for just as the arrows were about to reach him, each and every one was transformed into a beautiful flower. Through Hanuman's unwavering devotion to the Lord, even the Lord's wrath was transformed into a blessing. Finally Sri Rama had to admit defeat, overcome not by resistance but by love and acceptance.

Similarly, Amma says that our love for and surrender to our guru should be so great that we can accept even the guru's discipline as a wonderful blessing.

The beginning of Devi Bhava is not the only time arati is performed to Amma; it is also done after the evening bhajan and during the *pada puja* (ritual bathing of the guru's feet) that is performed as Amma enters the hall for each program. On these occasions the arati is done each time by a different devotee or group of devotees. During the pada puja, the swamis stand behind Amma and chant Vedic mantras while the devotees ceremonially bathe Amma's feet and perform the arati. A few days after Amma had asked me not to do the Devi Bhava arati anymore, I was following Amma as she entered a program hall to begin the morning darshan. The devotee who was to perform the arati to Amma for the first time was suddenly overcome by anxiety. His hands started shaking violently and he spilled the burning camphor on the ground. In the rush to put out the flame, it seemed that no one was going to perform the arati. In order to avoid a break in tradition, I leapt forward and took the arati tray from the devotee, who was by this time looking like he would rather be anywhere else in the world. As the other swamis finished chanting the verses, I performed the arati to Amma. In fact, a similar incident occurred two more times on that tour, which removed the last traces of sorrow within me over the arati affair. Even when Amma asks us to do something we don't want to do, her motherly love and divine grace will soften the blow.

Some years ago a Westerner joined the ashram as a brahmachari. For whatever reason, he decided that he would like to spend all his time with the Indian brahmacharis and avoid mingling with other Westerners as much as possible. He stayed in a room with Indian brahmacharis, ate with Indian brahmacharis and did his seva also with the Indians. Whole days would pass wherein he would not even speak to another Westerner, despite the fact that there were several hundred staying at the ashram. One morning, as he stood up from his breakfast of Indian food, surrounded by his Indian brothers, he thought to himself with a great deal of satisfaction, "Ah... my life is perfect! I get to spend all my time with senior Indian ashram residents who are such good influences on me, and I never have to interact with the Westerners at all." Not forty-five minutes later, the young man got the message that Amma was asking to see him. It was the first time she had ever done this, and he ran to her with great anticipation. When he knelt down in front of her, she asked him sweetly, "Would you mind working in the International Office?" This is the ashram's foreign office, which provides accommodation, administration and troubleshooting for all of the ashram's international visitors. With that one sentence of Amma's, the young man's "perfect life" was turned upside down.

In nature, we find that the mother birds often push their babies out of the nest in order to teach them to fly. Likewise, the spiritual master sometimes gives us difficult experiences in order to help us develop our strength. But just as the mother bird only nudges the baby bird out on its own when she feels confident it is ready, the spiritual master will not put us in a situation we cannot handle. Sometimes, struggles are exactly what we need in our life. If we were allowed to go through our life without any obstacles, we would not be as strong as we could have been. Many of our talents will manifest only when there is struggle, or when the need arises. If we are never put to the test, our inherent talents and abilities will be stifled.

Amma has said countless times that she neither desires nor needs anything from us. Her only wish is that we transcend the limitations within ourselves in order to come to a state of true happiness. We may think at times that we are serving Amma, but actually, she is the one serving us. She is already full and complete, needing nothing from anyone in order to be happy. But out of her compassion, she wants to bring all of us to that state as well.

Of course, it is not only the ashram residents who have been transformed by Amma. Take, for example, the villagers living in the vicinity of the ashram. Readers of *Ultimate Success* may remember the story of Amma throwing prasad to the villagers as she left the ashram for a foreign tour. At that time, the villagers did not come out of their homes to see Amma pass by and simply left the prasad candies lying there on the ground—only the children were interested. In recent times, however, we see a very different scene.

When Amma left the ashram for her 2005 European tour, as usual the ashram residents lined the path from Amma's room to the beach road. But this time, the path did not end there—even at that early hour it seemed the entire village was awake and standing in front of their homes with palms joined.

Lamps were lit in front of many houses, and the entire household—mothers, fathers, children, grandparents—had already taken their bath and waited near the lamps for Amma to pass by. The mantra *Om Amriteswaryai Namah* pulsed softly in tune with the waves crashing against the shore.

Amma's car moved slowly along the road, stopping at each lit lamp. The villagers stretched out their hands, and Amma pressed candies into them. After Amma passed, many of the villagers could be seen shedding tears. Some still chanted Amma's name; others softly murmured, their voices choked with emotion. "She touched my hand… she gave me a sweet." Others stood silently, motionlessly, blinking back tears.

Many people heard the mantras and ran straight from their beds in time to catch a precious glimpse of Amma, while others came straight from the bathroom, their clothes wet and hair still dripping. The scene reminded me of a story Amma often recounts about the gopis of Vrindavan. Once, the gopis heard that Sri Krishna was going to dance on the banks of the Yamuna River. Hearing this, they all dropped what they were doing and immediately ran out of their houses. Some of them had been in the midst of applying their eyeliner and had finished only one eye. Others had their anklets tied only on one ankle. Those who had been working in the kitchen looked terrible, having unwittingly wiped their faces with their soot-covered dirty hands. The gopi who had been serving lunch to her husband came running out with a ladle in her hand, while another gopi, who had been sweeping the yard when she heard the call, still held a broom in her hand. The mere mention of the Lord's name was enough for the gopis to drop all their work and run toward the banks of the river Yamuna.

Regarding the transformation in the behavior and attitude of the locals around Amma's ashram, a villager who works as a soldier commented, "Before the tsunami, we all believed Kadal Amma (Mother Sea) was our protector. But when the sea set out to destroy us, it was Amma who protected us. Amma is greater than Mother Sea."

Only days earlier, the villagers had lined the streets for Amma in honor of her 52nd birthday. Again, this was a departure from the past. This year was the first time they had taken Amma's birthday as a holiday. None of the fishermen had gone out to sea that day. More than taking the day off, it signaled a marked difference in the villagers' attitude toward Amma. After all that she has done for them in the wake of the devastating tsunami, it is no surprise that they have chosen to consider the day of Amma's birth as a "holy day." These were the very same people who used to throw stones and hurl insults at Amma and for many years refused to set foot in the ashram.

Recently, the father of a child enrolled in Amrita Vidyalayam (Amma's system of primary schools) came for Amma's darshan. He was having obvious difficulty in holding back his emotion, and as soon as he fell into Amma's arms, he began to sob. As it happened, these were not tears of sorrow but gratitude and joy.

A few days before, he had been invited to his son's school to take part in a program that all of Amma's schools have been conducting for several years now. In order to help instill the children's respect and love for their parents, the ashram schools organize mass ceremonies wherein the children ceremonially bathe their parents' feet. The traditional worship is based on the injunction given in the *Taittiriya Upanishad* (1.11.2): "May the mother be, to thee, a god. May the father be, to thee, a god."

The man looked up into Amma's eyes. "When my son began to wash my feet, I asked myself, 'Who am I to be worshipped like this? I am not worthy of such a thing.'" He then told Amma that in his entire life he had not once touched his parents' feet, much less performed pada puja to them.

But then, the man told Amma, when he returned home, he felt so inspired from his child's actions that the next time he saw his own mother, he quickly fell at her feet in reverence for all she had done for him throughout his life.

"When I touched my mother's feet, she couldn't believe it," the man said. "Now, for the first time in thirty-six years, I am respecting and loving my mother. Only when I bowed down to her did I come to know her value. My mother then, with love and affection, blessed me, saying, 'Whatever bad feelings I may have held toward you are nullified by this.'"

The man then thanked Amma profusely for helping to re-establish traditional values in the coming generation. "Amma, you have taught me the greatness of motherhood. I will be indebted to you always. You are the mother of all."

When Amma visited a Tamil tsunami relief camp in Sri Lanka in February 2005, a group of Tamil Tigers—members of the LTTE (Liberation Tigers of Tamil Eelam)—came for Amma's darshan, as did a group of soldiers from the Sinhalese government's Special Task Force (STF). The Sinhalese and Tamil armies have been engaged in a brutal civil war since 1983, in which more than 60,000 people have been killed.

Many of the members of the LTTE who came for Amma's darshan were young women, recognizable as militants by their short haircuts, men's shirts and wide black gun belts. As the ladies came before Amma, their hardened faces softened, and smiles lit up their eyes. Not sure that Amma spoke Tamil, they asked a government official who happened to be standing near Amma at the time, to translate for them. This was perhaps the most remarkable moment of all, for here was a group of militants asking for assistance from a representative of the government they had vowed to topple. The official was overwhelmed at seeing the two groups coming together without bloodshed or even a trace of enmity. "Amma is the unifying force," she said. "Only Amma can bring all these people together."

Such a transformation is possible only in the presence of a true master. Amma says that the greatest miracle one can perform is not to materialize an object out of thin air, as we cannot make manifest any object that does not already exist in creation. The greatest miracle, Amma says, is to create a profound transformation within the heart of a human being.

This is a miracle Amma performs every day of her life. ❖

CHAPTER 14

Talking to God

"Prayer does not change God, but it changes him who prays."

—Søren Kierkegaard

If meditation is silent communion with God, prayer is like starting up a conversation. Amma says that thankfulness is real prayer, but most of us pray with some request in mind; very few pray simply out of their gratitude and love for God, without expecting any benefit. Whatever our motive, however, the essential ingredient in prayer is faith. It is faith and intensity that makes our prayers bear fruit. Amma gives the example of sending a letter. Even if we apply the correct postage, without writing the address on the envelope our letter will never reach its intended destination. At present, even though we may claim to have faith in God, our faith is often very shallow. Amma tells the following story.

A man who lived at the foot of a mountain had a lover who lived on the other side of the mountain. Whenever he wanted to see her, he had to make a long journey around the mountain, as it was too high and treacherous to pass over. One day he remembered the biblical adage that one who has faith the size of a mustard seed can move mountains. Though he was not such a great devotee, he figured that he had at least *that* much faith, and every morning he would sit with his eyes closed, praying, "O Lord, please move this mountain so that I can see my beloved from my front yard."

After praying thus, he would walk out in front of his house to check whether or not the mountain had moved. This went on for several months, but the mountain never moved. Finally the man threw up his hands in defeat, shouting, "I knew it wouldn't move in the first place!"

In fact, real faith is very rare. There is a story about a village in India that was severely affected by drought for several years. After searching far and wide, the villagers found a priest who was renowned for his ability to bring rain through conducting an elaborate *yajna* (ritual). After making all the preparations, the big day finally arrived. Thousands of people gathered to witness the priest perform the ceremony, which was supposed to bring torrential rain immediately upon completion. Out of the throng, only one person brought an umbrella. It was a small boy. When people saw him coming, they asked him, "Why are you carrying an umbrella? The sun is not so hot today."

The boy replied with a question of his own: "Isn't it about to rain?" Even though the villagers had gone to all the trouble to find a priest to conduct the yajna, none of them believed that it would actually rain. However, the story goes that due to the innocent faith of this one small boy with an umbrella, the yajna was a grand success, bringing a torrential downpour upon its completion.

We never forget to call out to God when we are in need of assistance, but too often when a fortuitous solution appears before us, we fail to give God credit for answering our prayers. Once there was a woman who was rushing home from a doctor's appointment. The doctor had been delayed at the hospital, and by the time she left the clinic, the woman was running way behind schedule. She still had to pick up her prescription, pick up the children from the babysitter, get home, make dinner and then be on time to attend the parent-teacher conference that evening. As she began to circle the busy shopping center looking for a place to park, it started to rain heavily. While she wasn't the type to bother God with a small problem, she began to pray as she turned down the row closest to the front door. "Lord, you know what a day I've had, and there is still an awful lot to do. Could you please grant me a parking space right away, and while you are at it, could you make it close to the building so I don't get soaked?" She had hardly finished forming the words when she saw the reverse lights of a car come on at the end of the row. It was the best space in the parking lot, right next to the handicapped spaces and straight out from the front door of the shopping center. As she pulled into the ideal spot, she said, "Never mind, God, I'll take a rain check on that last request—something just opened up here without Your help!"

Amma says that a true seeker accepts every situation in life as a gift from God or the guru. Feeling and expressing gratitude to the Supreme Being for all that we have been given is real prayer. It is not that God or the guru needs our thanks or praise; it is for our own sake that we remember that everything we have is a gift. At least for the duration of our prayer, we will not be egoistic—we are submissive before God. Prayer naturally cultivates humility and helps us to recognize the limitations of our own strength.

In the final analysis, we are helpless. Amma says that even the power to lift a finger comes from God alone. If we can maintain a prayerful attitude at all times, we can become humble and thereby invoke divine grace into our life. Amma says, "Even if rain falls on a mountain's peak, it will not remain there; it flows into low-lying areas. Similarly, divine grace flows naturally toward one who has cultivated humility."

Amma says that while eating a piece of chocolate, we should remember the manufacturer of the chocolate—while enjoying creation, we should remember the Creator. Whatever experience we have in life, whether it is good or bad, is a result of our prarabdha. We don't mind having good experiences; we never complain about that. Similarly, when we have bad experiences, we should take comfort in the fact that we have exhausted that much more of our negative prarabdha. And we should always remember that there are others who are far worse off than we.

Once, a young man was at the end of his rope. Seeing no way out, he dropped to his knees in prayer. "Lord, I can't go on," he said. "I have too heavy a burden to bear."

When the young man opened his eyes, he found that his surroundings had changed. He was kneeling inside an enormous room, and God was standing before him. "My son," the Lord gently instructed, "if you can't bear its weight, just put your burden down inside this room. You can pick up any other burden you wish."

The man was filled with relief. "Thank you, Lord," he sighed, and, finding that his problems and worries had taken the form of a bundle over his shoulder, he did as he was told. As he looked around he saw many different bundles; some so large they would need several people just to pick up. After wandering around for a long time, he finally spotted a tiny bag lying abandoned in the corner.

"I'd like that one, Lord," he whispered.

The Lord replied, "My son, that's the one you brought in."

Sometimes when our prayers go unanswered, we may wonder if God is ignoring us or taking a vacation. But we should remember that God's perspective is much broader than ours. There is a story about an ant that was doing tapas to receive a vision of God. His plan was to ask God for the boon that whomever an ant bites should die. God knew that such a boon would be disastrous for humanity, but in the end the ant's tapas was so intense that God could not resist giving him darshan and offering him a boon. When God asked the ant what he wanted, however, He also made sure the ant left some room for interpretation in his request. The ant excitedly exclaimed, "Yes, my Lord, I have something in mind—whenever an ant bites a human being, it should die."

To which God replied, "Your request is granted—whenever an ant bites a human being, the ant will die." Then God disappeared before the ant had a chance to clarify his request. To this day, of course, an ant that bites a human being has a very short life expectancy.

Amma has often commented that it is only due to the fact that God does not answer all prayers that there is some harmony left in the world. Just think—the bartender prays for more customers, the doctor prays for more patients, and the gravedigger prays for a plague.

When mahatmas are not present in the world, everything takes place exactly according to the law of karma. A mahatma, however, has the power to alter our karma (to the extent that we have become fit to receive his grace). In this sense it can be said that mahatmas like Amma are even more compassionate than God. As Amma's devotees, many of us have the experience that even our simple prayers are answered. We might have been praying to God for a long time without receiving any response. But Amma grants our prayers very quickly even though we may not deserve it. If we ask her for something we desire—as long as it doesn't hurt anyone and it falls in line with dharma, she will definitely help us.

When we pray to an invisible God, it may be difficult for us to pray with much intensity. But when we pray to someone like

Amma whom we can see, hear and touch, we will naturally be able to pray with more love and faith. This intensity also helps in ensuring that our prayers to Amma are answered.

One of Amma's brahmacharis shared the following story with me. There's a Western devotee of Amma who's been coming to the ashram in India for several years now. Typically he goes on Amma's North India Tour, but one year he did not come. When he showed up the next year, the brahmachari asked him why he had not come the year before. The devotee explained that one day on his last tour with Amma, he had had the chance to sit next to Amma while she gave darshan and hand her the candy and packet of *vibhuti* (sacred ash) she was giving to each devotee as prasad. As the man was handing Amma the prasad, a lady about his age came for darshan. She seemed to him very beautiful and very much the type of girl he had been searching for his entire life. Now, remember, this is in India, so Amma was giving darshan to 30,000 or more people that day. As such, she was giving darshan very fast. As this man handed the next piece of prasad to Amma, he silently prayed: "Amma, why can't you find a sweet girl like that for me." At that very moment, Amma stopped what she was doing. She turned around and looked right into the man's eyes, flashed a brilliant smile and then went back to giving darshan.

The man did not think too much more about it. But as soon as he returned to his country, he met someone who very much resembled the girl to whom Amma had been giving darshan at that moment back in India. The man and woman began seeing each other, and soon they fell in love. Amma had fulfilled his wish.

The relationship went on for the better part of a year; this was why he had not come to India the previous year. But after some time, they began to disagree with one another about small things, and then the small things became big things, and before long they were separating due to "irreconcilable differences."

When we pray for Amma or God to grant us something we desire—a new car, a better job, a beautiful wife or a handsome husband—we should remember that all worldly things come and go, bringing as much pain as joy.

Before the Mahabharata War began, Arjuna and Duryodhana both went to meet Sri Krishna to request his assistance in winning the war. Arjuna went on behalf of the Pandavas, and Duryodhana went on behalf of the Pandavas' enemy, the Kauravas. Both men reached the Lord's house almost simultaneously; Duryodhana was just a few moments ahead of Arjuna. Both men entered the house and proceeded to Sri Krishna's bedroom where he lay sleeping. There was an ornate chair at the head of the Lord's bed; Duryodhana seated himself there. Arjuna, being naturally humble toward the Lord, stood with palms folded reverentially near the Lord's feet. Thus, even though Duryodhana entered the bedroom first, it was Arjuna that Sri Krishna saw first when he opened his eyes. The Lord asked the two men what they wanted.

Duryodhana, leader of the unrighteous Kauravas, said, "My Lord, I want your help in winning the war against the Pandavas. Since I got here first, you should take up my cause."

Sri Krishna was unruffled. "It's true that you came first, but it was Arjuna whom I first laid eyes upon. Thus I shall help you both. One of you can have my entire army with all its millions of soldiers, elephants, horses and chariots, and the other can have me alone. I shall not carry weapons, nor shall I fight; rather, I will be your charioteer. Arjuna is younger than you, Duryodhana, and it is said that the youngest should be offered the first choice. So we shall let Arjuna choose first."

"I will take you alone, my Lord," Arjuna said without a moment's hesitation. "You alone are my true refuge, and without you on my side, I wouldn't even want to win the war."

Duryodhana laughed mirthlessly. "It is my luck that my enemy is such a fool. Even if I had first choice, I would have taken your army, renowned to be undefeated in any battle. Adding your forces to my own, the Pandavas are sorely outnumbered, and I will surely win the war."

The rest, of course, is history. In spite of the overwhelming strength of the Kauravas' army, the Pandavas won the war.

Arjuna did not ask for material assistance; he asked only for the Lord's grace and guidance. In the end both prosperity and grace belonged to him, and Duryodhana was left with nothing—not even his life. It is also worth remembering the remarkable prayer of Kunti, the mother of the Pandavas and an ardent devotee of Sri Krishna. She would always pray to the Lord for only one thing: "O Lord, please give me more and more troubles, for only then will I be able to remember you." If we forsake God for the sake of the world, we will not necessarily get what we desire—we will get what we deserve. Without praying for our material desires to be fulfilled, let us seek God and his grace alone. Divine grace brings both material prosperity and spiritual evolution.

Of course, Amma always encourages us to pray for others and for the peace and welfare of the whole world. This cannot be considered a selfish prayer because when we pray for others, our mind becomes more expansive.

Once, a ship was wrecked during a storm at sea. There were only two survivors, who had managed to swim to a small, deserted island. There the two stranded sailors agreed that they had no other recourse but to pray to God.

In order to better concentrate on their prayers, they went their separate ways and settled down on opposite sides of the island. The first thing they prayed for was food. The next morning, a fruit-bearing tree suddenly appeared on the first man's side of the island. He was able to pluck its fruit and eat a hearty meal. The other man's half of the island remained barren, so he went hungry.

After a week, the first man decided he was lonely and prayed for a wife. The next day, another ship was wrecked, and the only survivor was a woman who swam to his side of the island.

Soon the first man prayed for a house, clothes and more food. The next day, like magic, all of these were given to him. However, the second man still had nothing.

Finally, the first man prayed for a ship, so that he and his wife could leave the island. In the morning, he found a ship docked at his side of the island. The first man boarded the ship with his wife and decided to leave the second man behind.

As the ship was about to set sail, a voice boomed from above. "Why are you leaving your companion behind?"

"My blessings are mine alone since I was the one who prayed for them," the first man answered. "His prayers all went unanswered. Obviously, he does not deserve to be saved."

"You are mistaken!" the voice rebuked him. "He had only one prayer, and that I answered. In fact, if it were not for his prayer, you would not have received anything."

"What did he pray for that I should owe him anything?" the first man demanded.

The voice answered, "He prayed that all your prayers be answered."

Amma always closes her programs with a prayer for the whole world. Recently, Amma has been asking her children to specifically remember those who have lost their lives or loved ones to calamity in various parts of the world. Amma's prayer embraces everyone—those who have died in the recent earthquake in Kashmir and Pakistan, the floods in Mumbai and in South America, the tsunami in Southeast Asia, the hurricanes in America, the stampede in Iraq, as well as those dying in wars and terrorist acts.

"The tragedies we are experiencing are not finished," Amma said near the end of 2005. "Nature continues to be angry and agitated. Only the cool, gentle breeze of divine grace can lift the clouds of anger, hatred and revenge. So let us pray with melting hearts." Many of Amma's devotees have commented about how correct Amma was when she predicted back in 2002 that 2005 would be a time of tragedy for the world and asked her children from around the world to gather for *Amritavarsham50*, Amma's 50th birthday celebrations, which took the form of a collective prayer for world peace and harmony. Amma frequently speaks about the power of group prayer. In the context of *Amritavarsham50*, where hundreds of thousands of people were gathered, she said that though we may all be like little candles, when we come together to pray for the peace and welfare of all beings, our light can illumine the whole world. ❖

CHAPTER 15

Sannyasa is a State of Mind

*To be satisfied with a little is the greatest wisdom; and he
that increaseth his riches, increaseth his cares; but a contented
mind is a hidden treasure, and trouble findeth it not.*

—Akhenaten, Egyptian Pharaoh

When we talk about finding the bliss, joy or peace within,
many people think that these are matters best left to monks,
and that without living in a monastery or an ashram there is no
hope to attain these states of contentment.

In fact, one of the lines in Shankaracharya's *Five Verses on
Spiritual Life* reads,

nijagṛhāttūrṇaṁ vinirgamyatāṁ

Leave completely and without delay your own home.

In the modern world, it is difficult to follow this instruction
literally. In earlier times, people were prepared from a young age
to move toward the goal of final renunciation, at least near the
end of their lives. The Vedas divide human life into four *ashramas*
(stages), and everyone grew up with the understanding that they
too would pass through each of these four stages.

The first stage of life is called *brahmacharya*, during which
the child would undergo education in a *gurukula* (traditional
boarding school). Apart from the academic subjects, the guru

149

educated the student about the goal of human existence: realizing one's identity as Brahman, the Absolute. The student also received all the necessary instructions for leading a harmonious life in the world.

After coming out of the gurukula, the youth would have a choice: pursue spiritual life wholeheartedly and become a *sannyasi* (monk), or lead a married life and take up *sannyasa* (monastic life) later in life. Sannyasa was considered a desirable path for everyone; it was only a question of timing.

Those who chose to get married and have children would proceed through two more stages of life before attaining sannyasa. The first is called *grihastashrama*—choosing a career, getting married and having children. This period allowed one to satisfy one's desires and, through experience, to gain mental maturity and purify one's mind through fulfilling one's duties and responsibilities as enjoined by the scriptures. Having received a good education during the period of brahmacharya, one used one's discrimination and finally understood that desires have no end and do not offer permanent happiness. Finally, when one's children were grown up and able to stand on their own two feet, one would be ready to enter the next ashrama, called *vanaprastha* (forest life).

In the vanaprastha stage of life, the couple retired to a solitary place (in those days, usually in the forest) and lived together as brother and sister. Relatively free from responsibility and having attained a certain degree of mental maturity, they were free to devote themselves to spiritual practices. Finally, they would enter the path of total renunciation—sannyasa.

In this context, we can see that Shankaracharya's instruction—Leave your home—is not so dramatic after all. It was seen as the natural course of a person's life. In today's world, however, without having been prepared to take such a step, we can look at this instruction from a different angle. We can interpret Shankaracharya's statement psychologically—while remaining in our home, we can cultivate an inner detachment.

Even if we were able to follow the instruction in the literal sense, we would still have to face the problems of the mind. We would still have to overcome our remaining mental attachments, likes and dislikes, desires and fears.

Amma says that the ochre color the sannyasis wear represents the burning of the identification with the body and the mind in the fire of detachment. It signifies a lack of desire for worldly achievements, and that one's whole life is dedicated to the realization of God, or the Self. But the cloth is only a symbol, a reminder of the goal. Some people have the level of detachment of a sannyasi even without wearing ochre robes. Amma wears only white, but her mind is totally detached. Ultimately, sannyasa is a state of mind. Many sages of the Hindu tradition used to live with their family, but internally they were real sannyasis. Amma says that the real meaning of sannyasa is inner detachment.

Once a married couple in the vanaprastha stage of life were walking together in the forest. Seeing a few precious stones scattered across the ground, the husband quickly kicked sand over them. His wife asked him, "Why did you do that?"

"I didn't want you to see the jewels," the husband confessed. "I was afraid that their sight would cause you to begin to long for the pleasures of the world."

"Are you still seeing those stones as different from any other pebbles?" his wife asked him.

Amma says that we should live in this world like butter floating on the surface of water—though it is in the water, it remains separate, detached. A boat can float on the surface of the water, but if water enters the boat, it will capsize. Likewise, Amma says that it is alright for us to live in the world, but the world should not live in us. Of course, Amma knows that cultivating this kind of inner detachment is not easy. She points out that throughout our lives, we are always leaning on someone for support. As babies, when we cry, our mother gives us milk. Of course, that is what she has to do, but thus begins our dependency on the outside world for comfort and solace. As children, every time we want something, we go to our mother, and she does whatever she can to satisfy our desires. As we grow up, we spend less time with our parents, but then we begin to depend on our friends for comfort and reassurance. Eventually, most of us fall in love, get married and have children, and so it goes. I have heard a story of someone who took this cycle of dependency even further. Her father had passed away when she was very young, and after her son was born, she went to see a so-called "psychic." The psychic told her that her father had reincarnated as her son. Hearing this news she ran home to tell her six-year-old son, "Oh, Dad, I'm so glad you're back!"

Some people argue that detachment means lack of love. In fact, it is only because Amma is not attached to anyone that she is able to feel equal love toward everyone. If we love someone, we become attached to that person and we become unable to feel the same degree of love toward others—all our love is concentrated on that one person or, at most, on a small number of people.

Amma has millions of devotees, and she looks upon each one as her very own child. Every minute of the day, at least one of Amma's devotees is undergoing some crisis or suffering in some way—they may fall sick, or they may get injured, or they may be suffering from financial loss. Ordinarily, when a child is in trouble the mother becomes miserable and cannot think about anything else. If Amma were to be attached to her devotees, she would be miserable all the time thinking, "My child is suffering," and she would not be able to concentrate on the work at hand or give happiness to those who are right in front of her. Of course, Amma feels and expresses sorrow when her children are suffering, but she doesn't allow the emotion to overpower her. In that way, Amma is perfectly detached. At the same time, she loves us all unconditionally and eternally.

At the most, our own biological mother may dedicate her very life to our happiness and welfare. In the end, she will pass away, take another birth and have a whole new family. At that time we will mean nothing to her—we will be entirely forgotten. In contrast, Amma will never forget us. She has promised to lead us to the goal, and she is ready to take any number of births to do so.

We should try to live and love in a similar way. Amma says that ordinary love is like a pond breeding bacteria; when we are attached to someone, feelings like anger, resentment and jealousy will naturally arise within us. Whereas, Amma says, detached love flows like a river. A river cannot be blocked by a particular stone or log; it simply flows over, around, above or beneath. Even as we share love and affection with our children, our parents or our spouse and do whatever we can for their sake, we should remember that our True Self is not affected by whatever happens to them.

One day the great sage Adi Shankaracharya came upon a *chandala*[18] with four pet dogs. Shankaracharya asked the chandala to move aside so he could continue on his path.

Without moving, the chandala asked the sage, "What is it that you want to move from the path? This inert body, or the indwelling Self?" He continued, "O Great Ascetic, you have established that the Absolute is everywhere, in you and in me. Is it

---

[18] A low-caste person—at one point in time, considered "untouchable"— who tends to corpses in a cremation ground.

this body, made up of the five elements that you wish to keep at a distance from that body, also made up of the five elements? Or do you wish to separate the pure Awareness that is present here from the same Awareness that is present there?"

Shankaracharya immediately recognized his mistake. Bowing low to the chandala, he composed five verses on the spot, stating that whoever had exhibited such equal vision, even a chandala, was indeed his guru. When the sage had completed the verses, the chandala disappeared, and there, in his place, stood Lord Shiva.[19]

In the *Bhagavad Gita*, Sri Krishna explains:

vāsāṁsi jīrṇāni yathā vihāya
navāni gṛhṇāti naro 'parāṇi
tathā śarīrāṇi vihāya jīrṇāny-
anyāni saṁyāti navāni dehī

As one casts off worn-out garments and puts on new ones, so the embodied, casting off worn-out bodies, enter into others that are new.

(2.22)

It is the Atman that enlivens our body. We say, "my dear daughter," or, "my sweetheart," but if our loved one dies, do we still call their body "my sweetheart"? In truth it is the Atman we love, not the body. Otherwise, when the soul leaves the body, we would continue to love the body, but this is not the case—we burn or bury the corpse as soon as possible. One verse of a bhajan which Amma frequently sings (*Manase Nin Svantamayi*) says,

---

[19] Though the story has been told this way, some believe that in fact it was one of Shankaracharya's disciples who asked the chandala to step aside.

ētu prāṇa prēyasikkuveṇḍi yitratayellāṁ niṅṅgaḷ
pāṭupeṭunnuṇḍo jīvanveṭinnupōlum

ā peṇmaṇipōluṁ tavamṛtadēhaṁ kāṇum nēraṁ
pēṭiccu piṇmāṛuṁ kūṭe varukayilla

*For wich sweetheart have you been struggling all this time,
not even caring for your life? Even she will be frightened by
your dead body and will not accompany you after death.*

A third way to interpret Shankaracharya's statement, "Leave your
home," is to understand that the "house" means the body, and
that we should gradually develop a feeling of detachment toward
our body and its needs. This may sound like an impossible feat,
but mahatmas like Amma clearly demonstrate that it is within a
human being's capacity to do so. It is not uncommon for Amma
to give darshan for twenty hours at a stretch without even getting
up to stretch her legs. As a young woman exiled from her parents'
house, she lived out of doors under the pouring rain and scorching
sun for several years. Once she survived only on tulasi leaves and
water for six straight months. Even after the first brahmacharis
came to stay at the ashram, Amma never used to bother about
where she would lie down to sleep. Sometimes she slept under
a coconut tree somewhere, sometimes behind the cowshed that
had been converted into the ashram's first temple, sometimes on
the sand by the backwaters. It was not an issue for her; she would
meditate or sing bhajans late into the night, and then she would
lie down wherever she happened to be at the time.

Even today, Amma does not pay particular attention to the
needs of her own body because she does not see her Self as con-
fined to a body. Rather, she sees her Self everywhere. Just as the

sky seen through a window is not bound by the window frame, Amma is not bound by her body.

At present, we give too much importance to the body; we want to spare it every difficulty. If, for example, our legs start to ache slightly while we are sitting in meditation, we don't think to make the effort to remain seated; we want to get up and go. Amma says that instead of worshipping the Atman, we worship the body; even when we go to the temple for a religious ceremony, we put on our make-up and dress in beautiful clothes. In another bhajan (*Uyirayi Oliyayi*), Amma wrote:

rudhirāsthi māmsattāl paritāpa durggandhappuriye samrakṣikkunnu

purivātil puṟamellām paripāvanamākkunnu purināthane aṟiyunnila

Protecting this pitiful city (the body)
stinking with blood, bone and flesh,
we clean the surface of the body alone,
knowing not its Lord.

Amma is not saying that we should neglect the body. It is our vehicle on the path to God-realization, and as such we should properly maintain it. But we should remember that our body is the means and not the end.

Many years ago, I was driving Amma's car during one of her tours of South India. The other ashram vehicles were far behind, and Amma asked me to stop and wait for them. It was about 4:00 p.m. and a very hot day. When the car was stopped, we all started perspiring. Noticing that drops of sweat were appearing on Amma's forehead as well, I asked Amma if I could turn on the air-conditioning. Amma answered, "No, it would be a weakness.

You are not going to die because you are sweating. If one is not able to go beyond such petty discomforts, how can one hope to face even more disturbing situations?"

Though we may not be able to transcend our body-consciousness, we should train ourselves to be able to overcome at least the very basic pairs of opposites: heat and cold, comfort and discomfort, etc. It doesn't mean that if it is very cold, we shouldn't put on warm clothes—we have to know our limits and work to transcend the opposites within those limits. That said, we should not be too dependent on external situations. In summer, we complain that it is very hot, in winter that it is too cold, during the monsoon that it is raining too much. If we never stop complaining like this, when can we be at peace? Let us train ourselves to bear at least the little inconveniences.

Many people think that becoming a renunciate means they won't have responsibilities anymore. Just before the Mahabharata War began, Arjuna asked Sri Krishna, who was serving as his charioteer, to bring his chariot to the center of the battlefield. There, Arjuna surveyed the enemy's camp and saw many of his close relatives and even his own archery master arrayed against him. Arjuna thought, "How can I kill all these people? It would be better if I became a sannyasi." It was Sri Krishna's advice to him at that time that forms the text of the *Bhagavad Gita*. After receiving Sri Krishna's divine counsel, Arjuna was able to fulfill his duty—going to war against the unrighteous Kauravas—with a detached outlook.

Once, a man with three children invited a sannyasi to visit his house. After giving him alms, the man began talking to the sannyasi about his three sons.

"My eldest son is a very clever businessman," he boasted. "Under him the firm has prospered so well that they have had to double their staff. The second one is working in another company, and he has worked so hard that it has tripled its previous profits."

"What about your third son?" the sannyasi politely inquired, and the real motive behind the father's invitation became clear.

"He is a good-for-nothing goose," the man confessed ruefully. "He has failed pitifully in every endeavor he has undertaken. In fact, I was wondering if you could take him away and make him your disciple."

Just as Arjuna was tempted to do, many people seek refuge in renunciation out of despair and to escape life's problems. Still others think that only those who fail in life should become renunciates. Both are incorrect. Renunciation is not for people who are lazy or want to avoid their responsibilities but for those who have a genuine longing to realize the Truth, and have realized that worldly comforts, achievements and relationships are not going to help them reach their goal.

Amma tells the following story to illustrate the real meaning and power of sannyasa. Once a spiritual seeker approached a wandering mahatma and asked him what it meant to be a sannyasi. The mahatma did not answer but immediately dropped the bundle he had been carrying and kept walking. Not satisfied with this answer, the seeker chased after the mahatma, crying, "Wait! You didn't answer my question!"

In response, the mahatma turned and walked back to the bundle and slung it back over his shoulder. Remaining silent, he continued to walk in the direction he had been heading.

The persistent seeker followed the mahatma and begged him to explain the significance of his actions. Finally the mahatma stopped and spoke. "When I dropped the bundle, it signified renouncing attachment to all the objects and people of the world. When I picked it up again, it signified taking up the burden of the world upon my shoulder; only one who is detached can truly serve the world."

Becoming detached does not have to mean withdrawing completely from the world and its affairs. Amma gives the example of a bank manager or cashier in a bank. He handles more currency in a single day than he will ever earn in his lifetime. Yet he does not feel any attachment toward this money because it does not belong to him. In the same way, a surgeon operates on hundreds of patients each year, and he does his best to improve the health or save the life of each one. He counsels and consoles their loved ones, but he does not feel attachment to any of them. If he did, his life would be miserable; he would be wracked by guilt and anxiety. When dealing with loved ones, we should try to maintain a similar attitude of detachment. Like the bank manager and the doctor, let us try our best to help others and bring happiness into their lives without becoming overly attached to or dependent upon them. In this way we can cultivate the sannyasi's state of mind even while remaining in the world—fulfilling our responsibilities and caring for our loved ones without sacrificing our inner peace. ❧

CHAPTER 16

"*Stop Not till the Goal is Reached!*"

Nor shall derision prove powerful against those who listen to humanity or those who follow in the footsteps of divinity, for they shall live forever.

—Kahlil Gibran

There is a story about the poet Rabindranath Tagore. One night, while staying on a houseboat, he was reading by candlelight. He need not have lit a candle; the full moon was illuminating the sky and the waters around him, but the poet, deeply engrossed in a book, failed to notice his surroundings. The night was pervaded by a deep stillness, broken only occasionally by the flap of a bird's wings as it passed over his boat or the splash of water as a fish leapt above the surface of the lake.

Finally, exhausted, he blew out the candle. Doing so, he was suddenly struck by the natural beauty of his surroundings. The pale yellow glow of the candle had been keeping out the moon's brilliant silver beams. A fish jumped, and he looked out to see it splashing back into the water. A few white clouds drifted through the sky and reflected onto the surface of the still, silver waters.

"What a fool I have been!" Tagore murmured to himself. "I have been searching in books for beauty, and all the while beauty was knocking at my door, waiting to be let in. Searching for beauty with the light of a candle, I kept the moonlight at bay."

In the same way, Tagore realized, it is the pale, flickering light of our ego that prevents us from being bathed in the brilliant light of God. All we need do is blow out the candle of the ego, step out of the cabin of our selfish desires, and see the beauty of God in all its glory.

About twenty years ago, a Westerner came to the ashram. We were all eating together in the small dining room. After the meal, I took Amma's plate and went to wash it in the kitchen. Normally in India, after eating we wash the plates outside the kitchen because the plates we have eaten off of are considered impure until washed; the kitchen, where food is prepared, must remain pure. But this Westerner, seeing me wash Amma's plate, came to wash his plate as well. I politely explained that plates must be washed outside the kitchen, that I was washing only Amma's plate in the kitchen. He said he preferred to wash his plate in the kitchen as well. Again I asked him to go outside, explaining that Amma was our guru and not an ordinary person—that she was always in a state of awareness of the Absolute and thus it was alright for me wash her plate in the kitchen. He replied brusquely, "I am the Absolute, too. What is the difference between her and me? I'm going to wash my plate here!" This strong reaction on his part was in itself a clear indication of his immaturity and egoism. Even though he was claiming, "I am Brahman," he was in fact clearly identified with his body, mind and intellect.

Amma says, "The subtlety of the Truth cannot be understood and assimilated without the help of spiritual practice." If we go on saying, "I am Brahman," without putting in the necessary practice to assimilate this truth, we are just like the man who boasted that he could see even in pitch darkness.

"If that is so," someone asked him, "Why do we sometimes see you carrying a light through the streets?"

"Only to prevent other people from colliding with me," the man declared.

Amma tells the story of the pundit who constantly repeated, "I am Brahman, I am Brahman," until someone dared to prick him with a needle from behind. Furious, the pundit began beating and cursing the "culprit."

In contrast, there is the famous story of Sadashiva Brahmendra, a mahatma who composed the beautiful song, "*Sarvam Brahmamayam*," or, "Everything is Brahman." This exalted sage from Tamil Nadu would always wander naked through the streets, his mind immersed in the bliss of the Self. One day he wandered into the king's palace as the king was holding court with all his noblemen gathered around him. The king, taking the mahatma to be a derelict, took his nudity as an insult to the crown and ordered him to cover himself. The mahatma did not even bat an eye, let alone make an attempt to cover his naked body—he took no notice at all of his surroundings.

When Sadashiva Brahmendra did not respond to his orders, the king blocked the mahatma's path, drew his sword and chopped off one of the mahatma's arms. The king was sure this would be a lesson he would never forget. Instead, the mahatma, noticing merely that it would not be possible for him to continue in that direction, reacted only by calmly turning around and beginning to walk in the other direction.

When the king saw the so-called derelict's response to his violent assault, he realized that he had just attacked a mahatma. Horrified by his mistake, he thought to himself, "As a king, it is my duty to protect my subjects, and here I have just attacked one of the most precious among them." With the intention of taking his own life as a penance, the king rushed after the mahatma with the severed arm in one hand and his sword in the other. Reaching him, he bowed down and clutched the mahatma's feet, shedding profuse tears and sobbing loudly.

The king's intense remorse succeeded in attracting Sadashiva Brahmendra's attention, where the attack by sword had not. "What is bothering you?" he asked the king.

The king held up the sage's severed arm and offered it to him, saying, "O Blessed One, forgive this ignorant fool who has done Your Holiness such great harm."

"No one has inflicted harm, and no one has been harmed," the mahatma replied. So saying, he accepted the king's offering of his severed arm and proceeded to re-attach it to his body. Waving his other hand over the wound, his body was instantly made whole. This is no mere fairytale—it happened just over 200 years ago, around the time of the American Revolution, and the accounts of many eyewitnesses are recorded in the history books of Tamil Nadu. In the end, it was a turning point in the life of both the mahatma and the king—the king renounced the throne in favor of a life of renunciation, and the mahatma gave up his wandering in order to prevent others from unwittingly incurring *papa* (demerit, or sin) by attacking him. Clearly, the sage's statement, "Everything is Brahman," was not mere words but his own incontrovertible experience.

Similarly, when Amma says, "I am Love; an uninterrupted stream of love flows from me toward all beings," these are not mere words—we can see this reflected in all of her actions. During darshan, her body endures all sorts of physical strain. People squeeze her, lean on her, kneel on her feet, but Amma never gets angry with them. She does not even express the pain or discomfort they cause her, lest they should feel guilty or hurt. Amma gives darshan to thousands of people every day and every person, right up to the last one, receives the same love. Amma says that everything she does—her every thought, word and action—springs from the overflowing love she feels for us. Amma is full of kindness and love even for those who have wanted her dead. This shows that Amma is established in what she says: "I am Love."

A man once asked Amma: "Amma, after I receive a mantra from you, what should I do next?"

"Chant it regularly with devotion and sincerity," Amma replied.

"And then?" the man asked.

"You will develop a certain capacity of concentration," Amma said.

"And what will happen then?" the man pressed.

"You will be able to withdraw your mind from your surroundings and meditate for a long time," Amma answered patiently.

"And then?"

"You can attain *samadhi*."[20]

"What will happen then?"

"First reach that level," Amma said. "Then you can come back and ask about the next steps."

This man had only an intellectual curiosity about spiritual life; he had hardly any intention to practice.

Amma says that one of the most important traits for a spiritual aspirant is a burning desire to realize the Truth. A man whose clothes have caught fire will not ask the passersby, "What shall I do?"—he will rush to any water, whether clean or dirty, he does not care. We should have this same feeling of urgency, the burning desire to know God. A lukewarm attitude will not help us to progress. Longing for liberation is like swimming against the current in a river. All other desires push us constantly in the direction of the current. Our mind never allows us to be still. If

---

[20] Samadhi is a transcendental state in which one loses all sense of individual identity.

we try to sit in silence without moving, the mind revolts, protesting, "Why should I sit here in one place when there are so many interesting things to do and enjoy? Don't be stupid! Get up!" The mind cannot stand being restrained. If we try to control it, it resists and revolts.

A horse wearing blinders can look only forward. Similarly, as spiritual seekers, our environment should not distract us; we should keep our mind always on the goal. Only if we can cultivate *lakshya bodha* (intent to reach the goal) will we be consistent in our quest and our every action become a sadhana.

We cannot say this is impossible—if we look closely, we will see that we already have the ability to remain aware of and focused on a particular goal. For example, there is a lady devotee who often comes for my programs in a particular city in India. She used to laugh hysterically at even the smallest joke. Then one day, while giving a talk there, I noticed that she did not laugh once even though I made several jokes that evening. This went on for the next few days. No matter what the topic, she always looked very serious. Curious about the change, when I happened to pass by her on the last day of the programs, I stopped and asked her what had come over her. She explained that she had just gotten dentures, and was afraid that they would fall out if she laughed. Even though she had wanted to laugh at my jokes, she told me, she had been controlling herself for fear of creating an embarrassing scene. Her goal was to prevent her new dentures from falling out, and to that end she was able to restrain herself from laughing. Likewise, Amma says that if we are aware of the spiritual goal of life and sincere about attaining it, we can exercise a great deal of discipline.

Speaking about the importance of a regular routine of spiritual practice, Amma says, "It is like an alarm that wakes us up.

There was a man who used to wake up at 8:00 a.m. each day. Once he had an interview at 10:00 a.m., but to get to the place where the interview was to be held, he had to wake up at 4:00. So he set an alarm and by doing so, he was able to wake up at 4:00. The alarm helps us to increase our awareness. Similarly, we need these basic rules and regulations just like a child attending primary school needs a timetable. Slowly we will be able to gain mastery over the mind."

Amma gives the following example: take a piece of wood and try to immerse it in water. Each time it comes back to the surface, push it down again. As soon as you let go of your hand, the piece of wood will float back to the surface. The wood will not stay under water, but as we repeat the action constantly, our muscles will develop. In the same way, even if we are not able to concentrate in the early stages of spiritual practice, just sticking to a schedule will help to discipline our mind and keep us on the right track.

Sometimes we stop our sadhana, feeling that we are not making progress. One may think, "I can't chant the mantra with concentration, so why should I continue?" Or, we hope to get some experience during our meditation and when nothing spectacular happens, we get discouraged. This attitude is not correct; we must persevere in our efforts. Amma gives the example of swimming upstream against a strong current—we may not move forward very quickly or even at all, but if we were to stop putting forth effort we would be swept backwards at a rapid rate. Likewise, at the very least, our sadhana prevents us from being completely drowned by our negative tendencies and selfish desires.

One of Amma's devotees who had been staying at the ashram for many years found that he was still unable to control his fiery temper. He asked Amma if he could take a vow of silence for one year, spending most of his time in meditation, and Amma agreed. For the duration of the year, though he lost his temper from time to time, he was not able to scold or shout at anyone because he did not want to break his vow of silence. At the end of the year, however, he started talking again and it quickly became apparent that there had been no great change in his character. After being harshly scolded by this man, one ashram resident complained to one of the brahmacharis, "For one whole year his only job has been to develop patience and kindness, and even in that he has failed. What's the use of all this *tapas* (austerity)?"

The brahmachari, however, chose to look at the bright side. "At least for that year, he did not bother anyone!"

Amma says that life on the spiritual path can be compared to taking a long-distance flight. When we are on the plane, we do not feel that we are moving at a great speed, but within hours we land in another country thousands of miles away. We should not worry if we lack concentration—we will at least attain the *asana siddhi*.[21] If we cannot bring ourselves to meditate or chant our mantra, we can at least read a spiritual book. The most important thing is to cultivate a discipline, to sit for a fixed amount of time every day. Our sadhana should be steady and regular; it is not enough to practice once in a while.

To doubt whether Self-realization is possible is the biggest obstacle in a spiritual aspirant's life. The night before the Buddha attained liberation, he sat at the foot of the bodhi tree with the resolution, "Even if this body should dry up and wither away, I will not move from this spot until the ultimate wisdom dawns within me." Swami Vivekananda used to exhort his followers,

---

[21] Literally, "perfection in sitting." Asana siddhi is the third step out of eight steps to liberation outlined in the Patanjali Yoga Sutras. The first two steps are known as *yama* and *niyama*, or the do's and don'ts of spiritual life.

"Arise! Awake! Stop not till the goal is reached!" Similarly, Amma encourages us to be tenacious in our efforts and to never give up hope, no matter how many obstacles we encounter. "Along the spiritual path, there may be many falls, but if one does fall, the important thing is to not remain there, lying on the ground, enjoying the situation. You must get up and put forth the effort to walk further. Whatever effort you put forth on the spiritual path will never be wasted. To realize our oneness with God may take our entire lifetime—it may take *several* lifetimes. We just have to keep trying. There is no other way. Everyone has to tread the spiritual path today or tomorrow. If you come upon an obstacle, you have to surmount it."

From the sky come rain and snow. This rain and snow become a river flowing down from the mountains, carrying along with it many objects it encounters on its way, and finally merging in the ocean. If the river comes across a major obstacle, such as a large rock, the river may flow over the rock, or it may deviate slightly in its path, but it still flows toward the ocean.

The flow of life is not haphazard; just like a river, it has both a source and a goal. The source of all life is Pure Consciousness. The goal of our journey through life is to realize our oneness with this Supreme Self. Many foreign objects such as waste, driftwood and sand get carried along by the river but are not part of the essential nature of the river. They serve only to slow its progress. Similarly, we gather habits, hurt feelings, memories and desires in our journey through life. But all these are not part of our essential nature, and we will have to let them go before we reach the goal. ❖

CHAPTER 17

Hope for the World

"The world should know that a life dedicated to selfless love and service to humanity is possible."

—Amma

A shipwrecked sailor who had spent several years on a deserted island was thrilled one morning to see a ship offshore and a small rescue boat approaching. When the boat grounded on the beach, the officer in charge walked up to the marooned sailor and handed him a bundle of newspapers. He said, "The captain said you should go through these and read the latest news—then let us know if you still want to be rescued."

Over the past couple of years, Amma's focus on providing humanitarian aid has become greater than ever before. This was, in large part, dictated by the times in which we are living—Amma has been doing her best to relieve the suffering of victims of natural disasters in different parts of the world. In the summer of 2005, the United Nations designated Amma's ashram with Special Consultative Status in recognition of its extremely effective and far-reaching work in various fields of social service

Before the sun set on the day of the 2004 Asian tsunami, Amma was already providing food, shelter and medical care to thousands of displaced victims. Many readers may already know that soon after the disaster, Amma pledged to do $23 million worth of tsunami relief work, much of which was earmarked

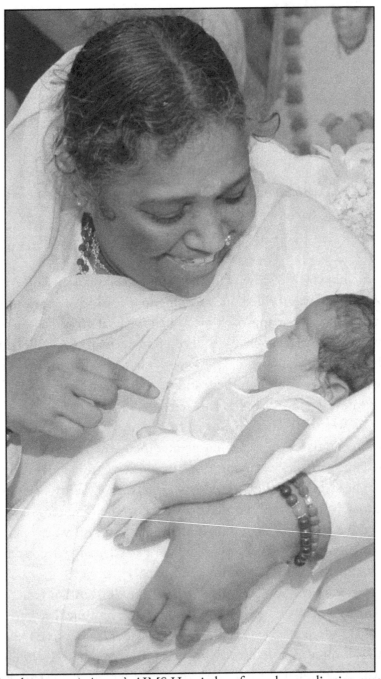

After the tsunami, Amma's AIMS Hospital performed recanalization surgery for seven mothers who had lost all their children in the disaster and had previously undergone tubal ligation. Amma holds one of their new babies.

for building 6,200 houses for displaced tsunami victims on both coasts of India as well as in Sri Lanka and the Andaman Islands. However, the government specifications for the houses were finalized only after Amma had announced the details of her relief package, and it then became evident that the cost would be double the originally projected expense. No financial support was forthcoming from either the government or from any other religious or charitable organizations, but Amma did not want to go back on her word. Instead, she took it upon herself to start from scratch and innovate ways to cut costs without compromising the integrity of the houses.

To that end, throughout Amma's 2005 summer tour—before and after darshan—she was constantly telephoning to India to give instructions on how to reduce costs on the raw materials and how to overcome all the obstacles her disciples were facing in the work. Sometimes she even called in the midst of giving darshan—even while keeping someone's head on her shoulder, she was talking via speakerphone to the construction supervisors, telling them things like where to buy the sand, cement and gravel, and how to get the water they needed. In some places the condition of the roads was so bad that the brahmacharis and brahmacharinis first had to repair the roads themselves before they could even transport the materials needed. As of this writing, nearly 4,000 of the promised 6,200 houses have been completed and handed over to the beneficiaries, and the construction of the remaining houses is well under way.

Some journalists have asked, "Is Amma rich? Where does she get the money for all of this?"

The answer is that Amma is not materially rich. But when measured in terms of love and compassion and knowledge, she is infinitely rich. Amma says whatever she has accomplished has only been made possible by the hard work of her children. Amma never asks for donations; she offers free programs wherever she goes, and there is no charge for her darshan. Amma explains that before starting a project she feels inspired to undertake, she never spends time calculating whether it is financially feasible or not. Whenever Amma feels the need, she commits to help, and by divine grace the necessary resources always materialize.

Some of the funds used for the ashram's tsunami- and other disaster relief efforts actually had already been set aside for other projects which Amma had been planning to initiate in the near future. Amma says the future is not in our hands; only the present moment is. Because of this, Amma felt that she should switch her focus from these planned projects to disaster relief, as it was the urgent need of the hour. When the needs of the disaster victims have been fully met, she will look once again to the previously planned projects.

There is an ancient Japanese story about a Zen practitioner named Tetsugen. In his time, the Buddhist *sutras* (aphorisms) were available only in Chinese, and Tetsugen had decided to publish them in Japanese. 1,681 copies of the book were to be printed on wood blocks in an edition of 7,334 volumes each; it was a tremendous undertaking.

Tetsugen began by traveling and collecting donations for this purpose. A few sympathizers gave him large sums, but most of the time he received only small coins. He thanked each donor with equal gratitude. After ten years, Tetsugen finally had enough money to begin his task.

It so happened that at that time a river overflowed, and widespread famine followed in its wake. Without a second thought, Tetsugen took the funds he had collected for the books and spent them to save others from starvation. Then he began his work of collecting funds from scratch.

Several years later, an epidemic spread throughout the country. Tetsugen again gave away all that he had collected to provide medicine for the sick.

For a third time he began fundraising, and after twenty years his wish was finally fulfilled in 1681. The printing blocks that produced the first edition of Japanese sutras can be seen today in Obaku Monastery in Kyoto.

It is said that the Japanese Buddhists tell their children that Tetsugen made three sets of sutras, and that the first two sets, though invisible to the eye, surpass the last one which is on display in the monastery.

By the late 1980s, the ashram had begun to grow larger both in residents and visitors coming for Amma's daily darshan, and it was decided that a larger darshan hall should be constructed. As the ashram was still very poor at that time, devotees gave what they could to cover the cost of the construction materials. However, at the same time, Amma was approached by the management of a nearby orphanage which was ailing financially and unable to provide quality care for the children there.

Hearing about the children's plight, Amma decided to divert the funds which had been set aside for the building of a new darshan hall to take over the orphanage. When Amma's brahmacharis arrived at the orphanage in May of 1989, the buildings were dilapidated and the living conditions were appalling. The food was lacking in essential vitamins and minerals, and there was no milk for the children. The dining hall was a small, dark room with a dirt floor which was always flooded during the monsoon season, forcing the children to stand while eating. The roofs leaked in several buildings, and many of the floors were irreparably damaged by years of flooding. There were no medical facilities, and many of the children's health problems had gone untreated. There were no functioning latrines.

Today, the orphanage has been completely rebuilt—every aspect of the children's needs, interests and aspirations is attended to. Amma's orphanage is also home to an excellent school where the children have the chance to become fluent in Sanskrit and English in addition to Malayalam, and to complete their secondary education. Quite a few go on to higher learning as well.

I used to wonder what it would be like for a former resident of the orphanage who had lived there before Amma took over responsibility for the facility to visit it today. Then, on Amma's 2005 European tour, a 29-year-old Malayali boy who had been living in the Netherlands since 1985 came to see Amma.

The orphan boy was nine years old when a Dutch couple adopted him and his sister from the Parippally Orphanage and took him back to live with them in the Netherlands. This was in 1985, four years before Amma's ashram took over the orphanage.

When the orphan boy, now a young man, decided to come to have Amma's darshan, he had no idea that Amma was now taking care of the orphanage in which he had been raised. He discovered this only by looking at information about the ashram's charitable activities during Amma's program. Seeing pictures of the orphanage as it exists today, of course, he could not recognize the place. But the name of the small town in Kerala where the orphanage still stands left no room for doubt. Seeing the pictures of a loving home providing such a high standard of education and care, the young man's breath was taken away. What had been for him a living hell had indeed been transformed into heaven for the ones who came after him. But it was not too late for this young man—heaven had come to Holland.

"Thank you so much, Amma," the grown-up orphan murmured as he lay enveloped in Amma's loving embrace. "I have so many bad memories of my time in that orphanage. I feel so happy to know that you have taken it over and transformed it, and now I believe there was a purpose behind my losing my parents and coming to live in Holland. It was fate. It was so that I could meet Amma here today."

All of Amma's humanitarian activities have been similarly spontaneous responses to those in need. In the mid-1990s, Amma was approached by a group of women from a nearby town saying that they were living in thatched huts. Some of the ladies had unmarried daughters living with them, and one of the girls had recently been assaulted by a prowler. Without a door they could close and lock, there was no way to protect themselves and their children from danger, especially the grown-up girls. Amma's response was to begin building free homes in the vicinity of the ashram, and in 1996 to inaugurate the Amrita Kuteeram free-housing project. To date more than 30,000 homes have been constructed toward the current goal of 125,000.

When other families told Amma they could not meet their expenses due to having disabled earners or other difficulties, Amma initiated the Amrita Nidhi pension project that now provides more than 50,000 pensions nationwide.

Similarly, the healthcare initiatives—the waiting list for a heart operation in Kerala used to be so long that many of the patients, even if they could afford the operation, would die while waiting. Now, many thousands come to Amma as their last hope, and Amma answers their prayers. Many ashram branches across India operate free medical dispensaries. Amma's Amritapuri ashram houses a charitable hospital that treats thousands every week. There is a cancer hospice near Mumbai, an AIDS care centre operating in Trivandrum, and a charitable hospital for the deeply impoverished tribal people living in the remote hill stations of Kerala's northern regions. Community outreach programs range from house calls for the terminally ill to neurological care camps and free treatment for epilepsy and diabetes. Amrita Institute of Medical Sciences and Research Center (AIMS) Hospital, Amma's 1,200-bed super-specialty hospital in Kochi, Kerala, is dedicated to providing quality care to all, regardless of their ability to pay.

The orphanage was the beginning of Amma's large-scale humanitarian work, but if we look closely at the many humanitarian services provided by the Mata Amritanandamayi Math, we can see that they are merely an extension of what Amma has been doing since her childhood—taking care of the old, the poor, the neglected, the suffering.

And no matter how vast the network of activities becomes, Amma remains firmly in the midst of those who need her love and compassion the most. Amidst all these achievements, Amma has never stopped giving darshan. Even if she has to stay up all night reading letters, conducting meetings and talking on the phone, she still spends her days caring for her children with her own hands. Inspired by Amma's example, thousands have dedicated themselves to serving the poor, the sick, the distressed; in this way, her hands have become many.

Some may wonder how Amma has been able to accomplish so much in such a short period of time. Part of the answer is that because of the unparalleled example set forth by Amma, her volunteers are simply more inspired and more dedicated than others might be. A member of one NGO in Tamil Nadu who was overseeing tsunami relief operations said with amazement that, of the dozen NGOs doing work there, Amma's organization was far and away the most efficient and most effective. Another part of the answer lies in the way Amma spends the money she receives. Because the administration of Amma's humanitarian work is an almost entirely volunteer operation, there is relatively low overhead. Beyond that, Amma has always been very concerned about minimizing waste at the ashram and throughout all of her institutions, from a single handful of rice to high-tech electronic equipment. In most institutions of comparable size, there can be seen a great deal of waste and unnecessary expenditure. But Amma has inculcated a strong conservation ethic throughout her organization. No one wants to take more than he needs for himself, remembering where the money is coming from and to whom it is intended to reach. No one throws out anything that can be used or re-used.

Recently one of the ashram residents bought some electronic equipment for the ashram's audio/video department. When Amma found out how much the equipment had cost, she asked the purchaser if it had really been necessary. Amma then told him that he should henceforth keep a log and submit to her weekly reports detailing how much time he had used each machine each day.

Nothing escapes Amma's attention, even down to the smallest detail. During Amma's 2006 North American Tour, one day after the morning darshan in her ashram in San Ramon, California, Amma went out of her way to walk through the kitchen at the house where she, the swamis and some of the California ashram residents were staying. As she passed by the compost bin, she stopped and reached inside. A member of the tour group tried to stop her, saying, "Don't worry, Amma—there's nothing in there."

"How do you know?" Amma asked, and fished out what appeared to be a perfectly good piece of bread. Examining it, she said, "Who would have thrown this away? We should always remember that many people don't even get this much to eat in a single day. Especially an ashram, food should never be thrown away."

When Amma's Amrita University began to grow, Amma came to know that there was great deal of food waste generated at the students' dining hall. Amma addressed the issue when she had a chance to address them en masse; overnight, the food waste was drastically reduced.

Amma has always told us: when you waste food, remember the millions of children who will not get even one meal today. When you spend money unnecessarily, remember those who suffer in agony because they cannot even afford a single painkiller. Then she always emphasizes that we should remember where the ashram's money comes from. For example, there are some devotees that work in a granite quarry about 200 miles north of the ashram. They don't even have enough money to readily come to the ashram; yet, upon receiving their weekly wages, they dash off to make it to the post office before it closes. When their boss asks them why they are in such a rush, they respond, "We want to post a percentage of our wages to Amma."

Some years ago a poor couple from another district of Kerala came to the ashram with a huge sack of rice in their arms. Some brahmacharis helped them carry the sack of rice, and brought the poor couple for Amma's darshan. Presenting Amma with the rice, they told her, "We own a lottery shop from which we are able to eke out a meager living. Still, we have always dreamed that we could somehow take part in Amma's social-service activities. So we worked extra hours for the past three months; we even skipped one meal a day and saved money because of it. Though we desired to see Amma, we held back so that we would not spend all our money on traveling and have nothing to offer. After months of saving, we collected enough. On the way to the ashram, we stopped and bought a sack of rice. Will Amma please make use of this rice to feed the poor?"

Hearing their story, tears came to Amma's eyes. Service is not only for the wealthy; even the relatively poor can do what they can for those less fortunate. I am reminded of a beautiful story from the epic *Ramayana* that Amma often recounts to illustrate this truth.

After Sri Rama discovered that his beloved consort Sita had been kidnapped by the demon king Ravana and taken to the island kingdom of Lanka, the Lord set out to build a bridge to Lanka from the southern tip of India in order to rescue Sita. The bulk of the work was being handled by Sri Rama's army of monkeys led by his greatest devotee, Hanuman. However, the monkeys were not alone in their efforts. As the Lord was surveying the progress of the bridge, he noticed that a small chipmunk was darting back and forth from the bridge to the shore, scurrying between the legs of the monkeys who were carrying on their shoulders enormous boulders to add to the bridge. When he looked closer, Sri Rama saw that the little chipmunk's movements were not without purpose; just before reaching the mainland, the chipmunk would take a dip in the ocean, scramble up onto the beach and roll around in the sand. Then he would run back to the work-site and shake his body, depositing the sand onto the bridge. He carried out this ritual tirelessly, taking hundreds of trips back and forth. The monkeys were irritated by the chipmunk's presence and kept trying to kick him out of the way. "What are you doing here?!" one of the monkeys finally shouted.

"I'm helping build the bridge to save Sita Devi," the chipmunk answered.

All the monkeys in earshot laughed uproariously. "Nice try, little fella," they admonished him. "But how can you possibly help us? Look at the size of the boulders we are carrying!"

"It's true I cannot carry as much as you. But I am doing all that I can. I know that the Lord's task is a noble one, and I want to do my best to serve him."

The monkeys ignored the chipmunk and went on with their work. At the end of the day, they ran to tell Sri Rama about their progress. But he was not interested in hearing about their exploits—instead, he asked them to bring the chipmunk to him. "What could our Lord want with that useless fellow?" they wondered, but they dared not disobey. When they brought the chipmunk, the Lord picked him up and held him affectionately in his palm. "You don't realize, my dear monkeys, that without the sand deposited between the cracks of your boulders, the bridge would fall apart. Never despise the weak or the deeds of those who are not as strong as you. Each serves according to his own capacities, and no one is unnecessary." The Lord stroked the chipmunk's back with three fingers, drawing the stripes that adorn the chipmunk's back even today—an eternal reminder that God has a special love and concern for the small and the weak.

Amma has always said that it is not only the recipients of Amma's charitable activities who benefit—everyone involved in every step of the process benefits, either spiritually, materially or both. For example, Amma's devotees make different things—handicrafts, beadwork, greeting cards, flower garlands—and offer them to her. Because they do this out of their love for Amma and do not expect any reward for their labor, it becomes *karma yoga*[22] for

---

[22] Literally, karma means "action." Yoga means "union," and refers to the union of the individual soul and the Supreme Soul. Thus, karma yoga means to attain that union through performing selfless actions.

them. Amma blesses their gifts and other devotees then purchase these items as prasad. Amma closely supervises and guides those who distribute the money through the ashram's humanitarian projects to make sure that it goes to the really deserving people. Thus, those who labored to make the products as well as those who contributed the money to purchase the products receive punya, or merit, because the money is used to serve those who need it. At the same time, the recipients are able to benefit from the money—Amma's assistance often gives them a new lease on life. Finally, those who are distributing the money develop more awareness and discrimination. Amma says that if it is not done in this way, it is like doing *archana* (worship) without sincerity and devotion; we are simply transferring the flowers from one place to another place. But if we use the money in a conscientious way so that it benefits the most deserving people, it becomes worship. As Amma says, "God is not sitting up in the sky on a golden throne. God is present in every being and in every object in creation. Helping the poor and needy in whatever way possible is the real worship of God."

In the first days of Amma's 2006 North American Tour, a seven-year-old girl named Amritavarshini from Eugene, Oregon, came for Amma's darshan. As the child approached Amma, she gently placed a garland around Amma's neck. The garland was not made of flowers, but of dollars—$200 to be exact—everything the girl had in her savings.

As Amma held her, the child began to cry. She then gave Amma a letter she had written earlier that week with the help of her mother.

Dear Amma,

How can we cure sick people around the world? How can the world see that we are one in harmony and stop bombing each other? How do we make slavery and racism go away? It really puts me in deep sorrows. Please give this money to the world that is sick. Please take care of all the sick and the poor.

Love,
Amritavarshini

Amma told the child and her mother to sit by her side.

"Why are you crying?" Amma asked the little girl.

Fighting back tears, the child said, "I want to make peace for the world."

The girl's mother explained that about a week before she had come home to find Amritavarshini in tears. When she had asked her why she was crying, the girl replied that it was because of the slavery, wars, disease and poverty in the world. The girl then told her mother that she wanted to give all the money in her savings account to Amma to support Amma's humanitarian work. Her mother withdrew all but the minimum forty dollars required to keep the account active, but Amritavarshini insisted that even this remaining amount be given to Amma.

"Children like this are the hope for the world," Amma told everyone around her as she wiped Amritavarshini's tears. "We should fall down and prostrate at the feet of children like her. It is children like her who will change the world... May her innocent wishes come true." ❈

CHAPTER 18

Rising in Love

Human beings must be known to be loved; but divine beings must be loved to be known.

—Blaise Pascal

Though the farmer may want to cultivate a variety of crops, he always focuses on the soil, knowing that it is the substratum and deciding factor of the growth of all plant life. Similarly, Amma reminds us that whatever action we may be engaged in, we should always try to remember the Supreme Being. With that in mind, upon concluding our meditation, Amma often asks us to pray that our every action become worship of the Divine Mother:

O Divine Mother,
May my every word be in praise of you.
May my every action be worship of you.
May everything I eat be an offering unto you.
May my every breath be taken with the loving
remembrance of you.
May my every step bring me closer to you.
Wherever I lie down, may it be a prostration at your lotus
feet.

Amma says that the easiest way to transform our every action into worship is to perform the action with love. She speaks from her own experience—seeing the divinity in each and every

person and object in creation. Amma's love overflows into her each and every thought, word and action. It is this love that gives her such perfect concentration and transforms her every action into worship. As a rule, the intensity of our concentration and the quality of our actions is directly proportional to the love we have for the object of our attention. For example, while watching an interesting movie, we become totally absorbed and forget our surroundings and even our bodily needs; but if it is a bad movie, we feel restless and the movie seems to last forever.

Once, after a break-up, a man asked his ex-girlfriend to return all his love letters. "I have already given you back your ring," the woman protested. "What—do you think I am going to use your letters to sue you?"

"Oh, no," the man assured her. "It's not that. It's just that I paid someone twenty-five dollars to write them for me, and I may want to re-use them."

Have you ever wondered why we say "falling" in love, rather than "rising" in love? When we fall in love, our excessive attachment and sense of possessiveness toward the object of our affection causes us to lose our discrimination and make rash decisions that we regret later on. There is always an element of selfish attachment in our love, and the person we are in love with is usually attached to us as well. (If not, that is yet another cause of suffering.) However, when we have love for a true spiritual master, even though it may begin as an imperfect love full of expectation and attachment, the master helps us to transform that love into an unconditional and selfless love. Rather than falling in love, the master helps us to rise—in love—up to the heights of Self-realization.

Amma says, "Today's world believes the greatest relationship to be the relationship between a child and its mother. But in my world, it is not; the guru-disciple relationship is. When you understand spirituality, you become expansive. You lose your sense of 'mine.' *My* mother, *my* father, *my* child, *my* relatives… In the guru-disciple relationship, everything becomes 'Yours' (the Lord's). The 'I' disappears, and only the Atman exists. Love and serve others as your own Self. When the left hand is in pain, the right hand comes and consoles it. It is with this attitude that we must live life."

A few years ago, when Amma was in Geneva to receive the *Gandhi-King Award for Nonviolence* and address a summit of women spiritual leaders, there was an outdoor event wherein each of the event's participants was asked to hold a candle and stand in the grass in a particular formation so that the whole group seen from above would spell out the word, PEACE. As soon as Amma came down from the stage, however, her devotees circled around her, transforming the A into an unrecognizable morass. Amma strongly encouraged them to stand in their assigned places, but this was one instruction they could not bring themselves to obey. Wherever Amma moved, they simply couldn't help but follow. The other participants, of course, stood in their assigned spots and formed the letters perfectly, but Amma always seemed to have a thick orb of bodies surrounding her. At first, the event's coordinator was a bit frustrated, calling out in desperation, "People, people—we're trying to make a word here!"

But soon he saw that for Amma's devotees the attraction of being near Amma was greater than that of participating in the event. Finally, the organizer surrendered and decided to look at the reality on the ground. "Well," he suggested brightly, "Since you all seem to like circles so much, why don't you form the period at the end of the word?" When Amma heard this, she burst out laughing, and gamely led her children to the end of the other letters. After the event came to a close, a journalist who had watched the afternoon unfold asked Amma, "Do these people worship you?" Amma softly shook her head, pointed at everyone, and said, "No, it's the opposite. Amma is worshipping them."

To Amma, nothing and no one is insignificant. Her compassion is like an ocean, rushing forward to touch the feet of whoever is blessed enough to stand before her. On Amma's 2006 North Indian Tour, Amma's car came upon a drunkard, stumbling along the middle of the road. Amma told the brahmachari driving to stop. The drunkard passed by the car, swaying back and forth. As he passed the ashram vehicle stopped immediately behind Amma's car, he bounced against it, giving it a good whack before continuing on.

Amma allowed her driver to resume the journey, but after driving just twenty feet or so, she again told him to stop. She then opened her door, stepped out onto the road and called to one of the brahmacharis riding in the car behind: "He is fully drunk. Go and get him off the road. Make sure he sits down somewhere. Find the villagers and entrust his care to them." The brahmachari turned around and went back to attend to the drunkard in accordance with Amma's instructions.

There is a saying in Adi Shankaracharya's *Soundarya Lahari*: "May your far-reaching eyes—which are only slightly open like a blue lotus just beginning to bloom—bathe even a worthless, far-removed one like me in your grace. Just as the cooling rays of the moon fall equally on the mansion and the wilderness, it will incur you no loss, O Shive (Divine Mother, consort of Shiva), but this person will indeed become blessed."

Last year during Amma's European tour, Amma spent the night at her new German center en route to Finland. A converted horse ranch, the center is situated on the peak of a hill and provides a beautiful view of the surrounding village and the green pastures where the horses are allowed to run. In the morning, before departing for the airport, she came out to spend some time with the center's residents and to feed the horses. The morning was bright and clear.

After Amma fed the horses, she went back inside where she distributed prasad to the residents and other devotees who were gathered there.

"Last night, Amma thought she would spend the full day here with you," Amma said to the devotees, explaining that she had not known that she would have to leave as early as noon for her flight to Finland. "Amma had planned to do so much with you today—serve lunch, sing bhajans, go for a walk, outdoor meditation…"

"Give liberation…" a devotee added with a smile. The comment had been intended as a joke, but, as usual, Amma's response was profound.

"Everything Amma does is only for that," Amma said. "By spending all his time with the gopis of Vrindavan—playing with them, joking with them, stealing their butter and milk, what Sri Krishna was actually doing was stealing their hearts. This is what Amma is doing when she spends time with all of you. She is putting a special pearl deep inside of you, so that you will remember Amma everywhere you go, whatever you are doing.

"Normally when we begin a long, hard task, we will be tense the whole time. The only peace we get is when we think, 'I will get rest once the task is completed.' By providing the devotees with memories, deep inside they will always be thinking of Amma no matter what they are doing." Amma added that such thoughts—the moments when the disciple remembers being with the guru—are moments of peace and rest.

Amma then explained that in the path of *advaita* (non-dualism), one tries to see the whole world as an extension of oneself, and that in the path of *bhakti* (devotion) one tries to see the whole world as their beloved Lord, or guru. The two paths are not different, just slightly different ways of looking at the same thing. "In today's world, people run to hear talks on Vedanta, but here we try to *live* Vedanta," Amma said, referring to how she encourages her devotees to serve the world, seeing it as an extension of Amma, or an extension of their own Self.

"In reality, the guru-disciple relationship is the relationship between the *jivatman* and *Paramatman*, the individual self and the Supreme Self. In truth, they are one and the same. When standing on the shore, a river appears to have two separate banks, but in reality those two banks are one and the same at the bottom of the river. Once we remove the water [the ego], we will realize this truth."

Then it was time. Amma had to go to Finland. As Amma drove slowly off the grounds, it was a scene just like when Amma leaves Amritapuri in Kerala. Amma rolled down her window and held her hand outside the car so it could brush past the hands of all the devotees who had lined up along the driveway as she drove away.

Through giving us such precious moments to remember and contemplate, Amma has made our spiritual practice relatively easy. Worshippers of the formless Absolute and even most devotees of God would be hard-pressed to remember their chosen ideal as often as we can remember Amma. Whenever we see anybody wearing white, our mind rushes to Amma and the deep peace we feel in her presence. When we sit down to eat, we remember the meals Amma has served to us with her own hands. When we take a dip in a lake or a pool, we remember swimming with Amma.

When we see people dancing, the memory of Amma dancing in bliss wells up within us. When we engage in hard physical labor, we remember the times Amma led the way in the jobs no one wanted—from vacuuming a hall after a program to carrying bricks and sand all through the night. When we eat a Hershey's Kiss, we remember Amma's embrace. Soon after I met Amma, when I was working in a bank far from the ashram, whenever I would see vehicle registration plates of Kollam District (where Amma lived) or buses on their way to Kollam, I would think about Amma and forget myself. So many simple things can remind us of her. This is the advantage of having a living master. If we drop a stone in water, it will immediately sink. But if we first put the stone on a wooden plank and then place it in water, the stone will remain above the surface of the water. In the same way, if we take refuge in the true spiritual master, we can fulfill our worldly responsibilities without sinking into delusion, attachment and its attendant suffering.

Now that Amma has visited the ranch, everywhere the devotees look, they will see beautiful pearls—memories of Amma's visit. Amma has given similar pearls to her children all over the world. And though she was speaking to the residents of the German center, her instructions could just as well have been directed to her children all over the world: "Do selfless service thinking of Amma, and remember always that you and Amma are not two, but, in essence, one and the same." For Amma's children, this is both the path and the goal. From the very first step we take on this journey, we begin to enjoy a previously unknown inner peace. Even the desire to achieve liberation disappears as we rise up, like a phoenix from the ashes—out of our attachments, out of our regrets, out of our sorrow and fear—in love for the master.

Sometimes, while driving Amma across long stretches of India, I would wish that rather than driving from one definite place to another, I was driving through the infinity of space and I would never have to stop the car and move away from Amma's side; there would never be a break in my service to her. Similarly, as Amma takes us by the hand and leads us forward along the spiritual path, many of us find we don't even want the journey to end.

May Amma's blessings be with us all. ❖

Glossary

Advaita – Literally, "not two." Refers to non-dualism, the fundamental principle of Vedanta, the highest spiritual philosophy of Sanatana Dharma.

agami karma – The results of the actions we perform in our present existence.

Amrita Kuteeram – Mata Amritanandamayi Math's housing project providing free homes for very poor families. Over 30,000 houses have so far been built and given away throughout India.

Amrita Vidyalayam – Primary schools established and administered by the Mata Amritanandamayi Math, dedicated to providing value-based education. At present there are over 50 Amrita Vidyalayam schools throughout India.

Amritapuri – The international headquarters of Mata Amritanandamayi Math, located at Amma's birthplace in Kerala, India.

Amritavarsham50 – Amma's 50th birthday celebration, held as an international dialogue-and-prayer event at Cochin, Kerala in September 2003, with the theme, "Embracing the World for Peace & Harmony." The four-day celebrations were attended by international entrepreneurs, peace-makers, educators, spiritual leaders, environmentalists, India's foremost political leaders and cultural artists, and more than 200,000 people per day, including representatives of each of the 191 member countries of the United Nations.

arati – Traditionally performed near the end of a ritual worship, and consists of waving burning camphor before the object of worship. Arati symbolizes surrender—just as the camphor used in the ritual burns away without a trace, so too does the ego dissolve completely in the process of surrendering to the guru or God.

archana – Commonly refers to the chanting of the 108 or 1000 names of a particular deity (e.g. Lalita Sahasranama).

Arjuna – A great archer who is one of the heroes of the epic Mahabharata. It is Arjuna whom Krishna addresses in the Bhagavad Gita.

Ashrama – Stage of life. The Vedas divide human life into four ashramas.

Atman – The Self, or Consciousness.

AUM – (Also "Om.") According to the Vedic scriptures, this is the primordial sound in the universe and the seed of creation. All other sounds arise out of Om and resolve back into Om.

Aum Amriteswaryai Namah – Mantra that devotees use to honor Amma, meaning "Salutations to the Goddess of Immortality (Amma)."

avadhuta – Saint whose behavior does not conform to social norms.

Bhagavad Gita – "Song of the Lord." The teachings Lord Krishna gave Arjuna at the beginning of the Mahabharata War. It is a practical guide for facing a crisis in our personal or social life and is the essence of Vedic wisdom.

bhajan – Devotional song.

bhava – Mood or attitude.

brahmachari – A celibate male disciple who practices spiritual disciplines under a master. (Brahmacharini is the female equivalent.)

brahmacharya – Celibacy, and control of the senses in general.

Brahman – The Ultimate Truth beyond any attributes. The omniscient, omnipotent, omnipresent substratum of the universe.

darshan – An audience with a holy person or a vision of the Divine.

Devi – Goddess. The Divine Mother.

Devi Bhava – "The Divine Mood of Devi." The state in which Amma reveals her oneness and identity with the Divine Mother.

dharma – In Sanskrit, dharma means "that which upholds (creation)." Most commonly, it indicates the harmony of the universe. Other meanings include: righteousness, duty, responsibility.

Duryodhana – The eldest of the 100 Kaurava brothers. Usurped the throne to which Yudhishthira, eldest brother of the Pandavas, was the heir apparent. Through his hatred of the righteous Pandavas and his famous refusal to grant them even a blade of grass, Duryodhana made the Mahabharata War unavoidable.

gopi – The gopis were milkmaids who lived in Krishna's childhood home of Vrindavan. They were Krishna's ardent devotees. They exemplify the most intense love for God.

Gita Dhyanam – Literally, "Meditation on the Gita." Traditionally chanted before one starts studying the Bhagavad Gita, these verses exalt the glories of the Bhagavad Gita.

gurukula – Literally, "Guru's clan." Traditional boarding school where children live with a Guru who instructs them in scriptural and academic knowledge, while instilling spiritual values.

japa – Repetition of a mantra.

jiva, or jivatman – Individual soul. According to Advaita Vedanta, the jivatman is, in fact, not a limited individual soul, but one and the same as Brahman, also referred to as the Paramatman, the one Supreme Soul that constitutes both the material and intelligent cause of the universe.

jnana – Knowledge.

karma – Conscious actions. Also, the chain of effects produced by our actions.

Kauravas – The 100 children of King Dhritharasthra and Queen Gandhari, of whom the unrighteous Duryodhana was the eldest. The Kauravas were the enemies of their cousins, the virtuous Pandavas, with whom they fought in the Mahabharata War.

Krishna – The principle incarnation of Vishnu. He was born into a royal family but grew up with foster parents and lived as a young cowherd in Vrindavan where He was loved and worshipped by his devoted companions, the gopis and gopas. Krishna later established the city of Dwaraka. He was a friend and advisor to His cousins, the Pandavas, especially Arjuna, to whom He served as charioteer during the Mahabharata War, and to whom He revealed His teachings as the Bhagavad Gita.

Lalita Sahasranama – 1000 Names of the Divine Mother.

lila – Divine play.

Mahabharata – One of the two great Indian historical epics, the other being the Ramayana. It is a great treatise on dharma. The story deals mainly with the conflict between the righteous Pandavas and the unrighteous Kauravas and the great war at Kurukshetra. Containing 100,000 verses, it is the longest epic poem in the world, written around 3,200 B.C. by the sage Veda Vyasa.

mahatma – Literally, "great soul." Though the term is now used more broadly, in this book mahatma refers to one who abides in the knowledge that he is one with the Universal Self, or Atman.

Mata Amritanandamayi Devi – Amma's official monastic name, meaning Mother of Immortal Bliss, often prefixed with Sri to denote auspiciousness.

mukti – Literally, "Final dissolution of all sorrows." Refers to the liberation of the jiva (individual soul) from the cycle of birth and death. Occurs when the jiva realizes its true identity as the Paramatman (Supreme Soul).

pada puja – Ceremonial washing of the Guru's feet, or his sandals, as a demonstration of love and respect. Usually includes the pouring of pure water, yogurt, ghee, honey and rose water.

papa – Demerit accruing from unrighteous actions. The accumulated papa is the cause of sorrows in an individual's life.

Pandavas – Five sons of King Pandu and the heroes of the epic Mahabharata.

prarabdha – The fruits of actions from previous lives that one is destined to experience in the present life.

prasad – Blessed offering or gift from a holy person or temple, often in the form of food.

puja – Ritualistic or ceremonial worship.

punya – Merit accruing from righteous actions. The accumulated punya is the cause of happiness in an individual's life.

Rama – The divine hero of the epic Ramayana. An incarnation of Lord Vishnu, he is considered the ideal of dharma and virtue.

Ravana – A powerful demon king. Vishnu incarnated as Lord Rama for the purpose of slaying Ravana and thereby restoring harmony to the world.

rishis – Self-realized seers or sages who perceive the mantras in their meditation.

sadhana – Spiritual practice.

Sadhana Panchakam – Literally, "Five Verses on Spiritual Life." During the last days of his short life, Adi Shankaracharya was asked by his disciples for a summary of the essential principles of the scriptures of Sanatana Dharma. In response, the verses of Sadhana Panchakam dropped spontaneously from the lips of their master. The text comprises five verses each with four lines. Each line comprises two instructions or advices. Taken as a whole, the text is like a ladder with forty rungs, leading us to the kingdom of God.

samadhi – Literally, "cessation of all mental vacillations." A transcendental state in which the individual self is united with the Supreme Self.

samsara – The cycle of birth and death.

sanchita karma – The totality of the results arising from our actions in all our previous lifetimes.

Sanatana Dharma – "The Eternal Way of Life." The original and traditional name for Hinduism.

sannyasi – A monk who has taken formal vows of renunciation (sannyasa). A sannyasi traditionally wears an ochre–colored cloth representing the burning away of all desires. The female equivalent is a sannyasini.

Soundarya Lahari – Verses by Shankaracharya describing the "ecstatic beauty" of Devi.

satguru – Literally, "true master." All satgurus are mahatmas, but not all mahatmas are satgurus. The satguru is one who, while still experiencing the bliss of the Self, chooses to come down to the level of ordinary people in order to help them grow spiritually.

satsang – Being in communion with the Supreme Truth. Also being in the company of the mahatmas, listening to a spiritual talk or discussion, and participating in spiritual practices in a group setting.

seva – Selfless service, the results of which are dedicated to God.

Shankaracharya – Mahatma who re-established, through his works, the supremacy of the Advaita Vedanta philosophy of non-duality at a time when Sanatana Dharma was on the decline.

Shiva – Worshipped as the first and foremost in the lineage of Gurus, and as the formless substratum of the universe in relationship to the creatrix Shakti. He is the Lord of destruction (of ego) in the trinity of Brahma (Lord of creation), Vishnu (Lord of preservation), and Shiva. Usually depicted as a monk, with ash all over his body, snakes in his hair, wearing only a loincloth and with a begging bowl and a trident in his hands.

Sita – Rama's holy consort. In India, she is considered to be the ideal of womanhood.

Srimad Bhagavatam – Devotional text detailing the various incarnations of Lord Vishnu, with special emphasis on the life of Sri Krishna. Written by the sage Veda Vyasa after he completed the Mahabharata.

tapas – Austerities, penance.

Upanishad – The portions of the Vedas dealing with the philosophy of non-dualism.

vairagya – Dispassion. Especially dispassion toward all that is impermanent, i.e. the entire visible world.

vasana – Latent tendencies or subtle desires within the mind which manifest as action and habits.

Vedanta – "The end of the Vedas." It refers to the Upanishads, which deal with the subject of Brahman, the Supreme Truth, and the path to realize that Truth.

Vedas – Most ancient of all scriptures, the Vedas were not composed by any human author but were "revealed" in deep meditation to the ancient rishis. The mantras composing the Vedas have always existed in nature in the form of subtle vibrations; the rishis attained such a deep state of absorption that they were able to perceive these mantras.

viveka – Discrimination. Especially discrimination between the Permanent and the impermanent.

Viveka Chudamani – Crest-Jewel of Discrimination. An introductory text on Vedanta, authored by Adi Shankaracharya.

yajna – Sacrifice, in the sense of offering something in worship or performing an action for personal as well as communal benefits.

yoga – "To unite." Union with the Supreme Being. A broad term, it also refers to the various practical methods through which one can attain oneness with the Divine. A path that leads to Self-realization.

Yoga Vasishtha – An ancient text dealing with the philosophy of nonduality through stories. Traditionally attributed to the sage Valmiki, author of the Ramayana.

CPSIA information can be obtained
at www.ICGtesting.com
Printed in the USA
BVHW041734120620
581231BV00007B/287